THE WORLD OF...

Mathematics
SATs Revision

Andy Ballard

Contents

DIY fractions

A carpenter is tidying up his workshop. He has decided to make a rack for his masonry drills by drilling holes in a block of wood for them to stand up in. He needs to work out how long the block of wood has to be.

His five drills each have a different <u>diameter</u>:

$\frac{1}{8}''$ ('' means inch)

$\frac{1}{2}''$

$\frac{3}{8}''$

$\frac{1}{4}''$

$\frac{1}{16}''$

There will have to be a hole for each drill diameter and a gap of $\frac{1}{2}''$ between each hole. There will also have to be a $\frac{1}{2}''$ gap between the end holes and the end of the block of wood.

How long will the block of wood be?

First Jimmy must add the diameter of each of the five drills together: $\frac{1}{8} + \frac{1}{2} + \frac{3}{8} + \frac{1}{4} + \frac{1}{16}$

When adding fractions you need a common <u>denominator</u>.

The lowest number that 8, 2, 8, 4 and 16 all go into is 16.

So $\frac{1}{8} = \frac{2}{16}, \frac{1}{2} = \frac{8}{16}$ etc.

The <u>sum</u> becomes: $\frac{2}{16} + \frac{8}{16} + \frac{6}{16} + \frac{4}{16} + \frac{1}{16} = \frac{21}{16}''$

Then, there are four gaps of $\frac{1}{2}''$ and two $\frac{1}{2}''$ gaps at each end. This gives a total of 3'' to add on.

So: $\quad 3'' + \frac{21}{16}'' = 3'' + 1'' + \frac{5}{16}'' = 4\frac{5}{16}''.$

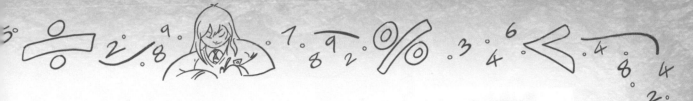

FURTHER PRACTICE

1 +

a) $\frac{2}{7} + \frac{3}{8} = \frac{16}{56} + \frac{21}{56} = \frac{37}{56}$

b) $\frac{3}{4} + \frac{2}{5} = \frac{15}{20} + \frac{8}{20} = \frac{23}{20} = 1\frac{3}{20}$

2 −

a) $\frac{4}{7} - \frac{1}{4} = \frac{16}{28} - \frac{7}{28} = \frac{9}{28}$

b) $\frac{3}{4} - \frac{1}{3} = \frac{9}{12} - \frac{4}{12} = \frac{5}{12}$

3 ×

a) $\frac{4}{7} \times \frac{4}{9} = \frac{4 \times 4}{7 \times 9} = \frac{16}{63}$

b) $\frac{3}{4} \times \frac{1}{3} = \frac{3 \times 1}{4 \times 3} = \frac{3}{12} - \frac{1}{4}$

4 ÷

a) $\frac{2}{9} \div \frac{1}{3} = \frac{2}{9} \times \frac{3}{1} = \frac{2 \times 3}{9 \times 1} = \frac{6}{9} = \frac{2}{3}$

b) $\frac{3}{8} \div \frac{9}{14} = \frac{3}{8} \times \frac{14}{9} = \frac{42}{72} = \frac{21}{36} = \frac{7}{12}$

KEY FACTS

When working with fractions:

↑ *adding and subtracting:* you need a common denominator first

→ **multiplying: just multiply across top and bottom**

← **dividing: turn the second fraction upside down and change to multiply.**

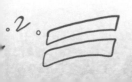

Spring sales

David and Victoria are trying to work out how much they are going to spend in the January sales. He needs a new jacket (usually £350) and a deluxe kitchen apron (usually £30); she needs a new pair of trainers (usually £120) and a body warmer coat (usually £12). They both expect a 15% discount off the usual, pre-sale price.

This is how David works out how much they will spend overall.

First he add up the amounts:

$$350 + 30 + 120 + 12 = £512$$

To work out 15% he does this:

$$15\% \text{ of } £512 = \frac{15}{100} \times 512 = 0.15 \times 512 = £76.80$$

To find the cost of shopping in the sales, he subtracts the 15% from £512:

$$£512.00 - 76.80 = £435.20$$

Victoria has seen her husband working this out and smiles to herself. She knows a quicker way. She knows that 15% off the original total price (100%) leaves 85%. So she just finds 85% of £512:

$$85\% \times £512 = 0.85 \times 512 = £435.20$$

In other words, a **decrease** of 15% is the same as finding 85%:

$$100\% - 15\% = 85\%$$

An **increase** of 15% is worked out like this:

$$(\mathbf{100}\% + \mathbf{15}\%) \times £512$$
$$\text{i.e. } \mathbf{1.15} \times £512 = £588.80$$

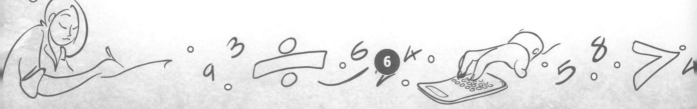

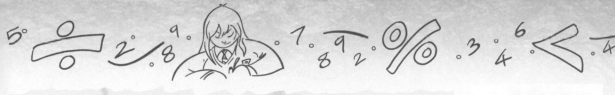

FURTHER PRACTICE

Look at these examples and answers and work out the missing ones.

1 Decrease each amount by the percentage shown:

    a) £450 by 10% $0.90 \times 450 = £405$

    b) 812 m by 20% $0.80 \times 812 = 649.6$ m

    c) 7.32 miles by 13%

2 Increase each amount by the percentage shown:

    a) $540 by **10%** $1.**10** \times 540 = \$594$

    b) 120 kg by **35%** $1.**35** \times 120 = 162$ kg

    c) 16.3 km by 14%

3 A car dealership bought a car for £4516. It is selling it for £4800. What is the percentage increase?

KEY FACTS

⬆ A *percentage* is out of 100, e.g. $16\% = \frac{16}{100} = 0.16$.

➡ To find a percentage *of* something you just multiply by the percentage in decimal form, e.g. 16% of $250 = 0.16 \times 250 = 40$.

⬅ To find a *percentage increase* multiply by (1 + the decimal percentage), e.g. increase 250 by $16\% = 250 \times 1.16 = 290$.

⬇ To find a *percentage decrease* multiply by (1 − the decimal percentage), e.g. decrease 250 by $16\% = 250 \times 0.84 = 210$.

⬆ Percentage change = (change/old value) × 100, e.g. 300 increased to 348: $\left(\frac{48}{300}\right) \times 100 = 16$.

Chocolate confusion

It's Sheena's birthday and she's just received a box of 24 chocolates. She agrees to share them with her friends.

She decides to:

- put eight chocolates aside
- share the rest equally among her two friends, her dog and herself
- share them so the chocolates last two days.

How many chocolates does each of them get on each day?

Sheena writes down this sum:

$$(24 - 8) \div 2(3 + 1)$$

Then she uses BIDMAS to work out the order of operations.

B	Brackets
I	Indices / Powers
D	Division
M	Multiplication
A	Addition
S	Subtraction

She does the brackets first:

$$(24 - 8) \div 2(3 + 1)$$
$$= 16 \div 2(4)$$

Then she **multiplies** the bracket by 2:

$$= 16 \div 8$$

Then she **divides** by 8:

$$= 2$$

So each of them gets two chocolates on each of the two days.

Sheena could have written it like this:

$$\frac{24 - 8}{2(3 + 1)} = \frac{16}{2(4)} = \frac{16}{8} = 2$$

Notice she hasn't done the division until she's sorted out the top and bottom.

FURTHER PRACTICE

Look at these examples and answers and work out the missing ones.

1 Find the value of each of the following:

a) $24 + 6 \div 3$ $= 24 + 2 = 26$

b) $24 \div (2 + 6) - 5$ $= 24 \div 8 - 5 = 3 - 5 = -2$

c) $6 + 3^2$ $= 6 + 9 = 15$

d) $\left(\frac{6+2}{2}\right)^2$ $=$

e) $(10 - 8)^3 \div (4 \times 2)$ $=$

2 Insert brackets so that each expression is equal to 12:

a) $4 \times 5 - 2$ $= 4 \times (5 - 2) = 12$

b) $20 \div 4 - 2 + 2$ $=$

3 For each part of question 2 above, calculate the value of the expression given without brackets.

KEY FACTS

☑ **Remember BIDMAS and what each letter means. It will help you remember the order of operations. Start with 'B' and work your way through the word in order.**

☑ **(Some people remember BODMAS instead, where 'O' is 'Orders / Powers'. This means the same as BIDMAS.)**

☑ **When addition (A) and subtraction (S) are together, it doesn't matter which way round you do them:**
$5 + 4 - 3 = 9 - 3$ **OR** $5 + 1 = 6$ **either way.**

☑ **Likewise when multiplication (M) and division (D) are together, it doesn't matter which way round you do them:**
$6 \times 10 \div 2 = 60 \div 2$ **OR** $6 \times 5 = 30$ **either way.**

☑ **It's when M/D and A/S are mixed together (along with brackets and indices) that BIDMAS is really important.**

Round and round

Kerry is shopping in France. She sees some jewellery that she likes and looks at the label – 28.60 euros. To work out what that is roughly in pounds she needs to make an <u>estimate</u>.

She knows that £1 is worth exactly 1.6 euros. So:

$$28.6 \div 1.6 \approx 30 \div 1.5 = £20$$

(The symbol ≈ means 'approximately equal to'.)
The exact answer to 28.6 ÷ 1.6 is £17.875

Look at the following estimates:

I know £1 is 1.6 euros, so…

28.60 euros

1   $126.5 + 4.8 \approx 127 + 5 = 132$.
The exact answer is $126.5 + 4.8 = 131.3$.

2   $16.5 \times 6.8 \approx 17 \times 7 = 119$
The exact answer is $16.5 \times 6.8 = 112.2$.

3   $36.8 - 4.4 \approx 37 - 4 = 33$
The exact answer is $36.8 - 4.4 = 32.4$.

4   $15.6 \div 1.5 \approx 20 \div 2 = 10$
The exact answer is $15.6 \div 1.5 = 10.4$.

5   A man's weight is 96500 g rounded to the nearest 50 g.
What could his actual weight be?

It could be anything between 96450 g and 96550 g.

(The man's weight could actually be up to 96549.999…g.
This is so awkward to write that we actually write 96550 g, even though we know this would really round up to 96600 g.)

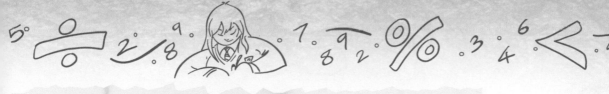

FURTHER PRACTICE

Look at these examples and complete the missing calculations.

1 Find estimates to each of the following calculations:

a) 14.8×3.1 $\approx 15 \times 3 = 45$

b) 123×6.9 $\approx 120 \times 7 = 840$

c) $10.8(63.8 + 78.2)$ $\approx$

2 A circle has a diameter of 14.6 m. Estimate its area (A) and circumference (C). (See pages 50–53 for how to do circles.)

$\pi \approx 3.14 \approx 3$ $d \approx 14$ or 15 $r \approx 7$

$A = \pi r^2 \approx 3 \times 7^2 \approx 3 \times 50 = 150\,m^2$ $(7^2 = 49 \approx 50)$

$C = \pi d \approx 150\,cm^2$

3 Each value below has been rounded to two significant figures. What are the maximum and minimum values for each?

a) 1200   Min 1150   Max 1250

b) 0.028   Min 0.0275   Max 0.0285

c) 5.0   Min   Max

KEY FACTS

⬆ **Estimating means rounding each number to an easily managed value that isn't too far from the original value.**

EXAMINER'S TOP TIPS

When you see the word 'estimate' in the question you MUST round the numbers.

If you work out the answer accurately you will get no marks.

Dicey decimals

Bart is terrified about next week's mental arithmetic test. Not only does it involve decimals but the students won't be able to use their calculators.

He knows there are four types of calculation that he should be able to do: adding, subtracting, multiplying and dividing. He also knows there are different ways to lay out the working.

The examples on these pages show a common way of working.

Adding/Subtracting
Put the numbers above each other, and make sure the decimal points line up.

8.43 + 7.26
$$\begin{array}{r} 8.43 \\ {}_1 7.26\ + \\ \hline 15.69 \end{array}$$

16.78 − 3.36
$$\begin{array}{r} 16.78 \\ 3.36\ - \\ \hline 13.42 \end{array}$$

6.57 + 7.24
$$\begin{array}{r} 6.57 \\ {}_1 7.{}_1 24\ + \\ \hline 13.81 \end{array}$$

24.67 − 5.18
$$\begin{array}{r} 2_1 4.6_1 7 \\ 5.1_1 8\ - \\ \hline 19.49 \end{array}$$

Multiplying
You don't need to line up the decimal points. However:

- When multiplying, put a **0** at the right-hand end of your second row before you start. If you had three rows there would be two **0**s to the right of your third row.
- Count the total number of decimal places in the numbers that you are multiplying, and make sure you have the same number in your answer.

8.43 × 3.5
$$\begin{array}{r} 8.43 \\ 3.5\ \times \\ \hline 4\ 2\ ^2 1\ ^1 5 \\ 2\ 5\ ^1 2\ 9\ 0\ + \\ \hline 29.505 \end{array}$$

Dividing

62.05 ÷ 5
$$\begin{array}{r} 1\ 2.\ 4\ 1 \\ 5\ \overline{)\ 6\ ^1 2.\ ^2 0\ 5} \end{array}$$

94.5 ÷ 2.1
$$\frac{94.5}{2.1} = \frac{945}{21} \quad \text{Multiplying top and bottom by ten.}$$

$$\begin{array}{r} 45 \\ 21\ \overline{)\ 945} \\ 84\ - \\ \hline 105 \\ 105\ - \\ \hline 0 \end{array}$$

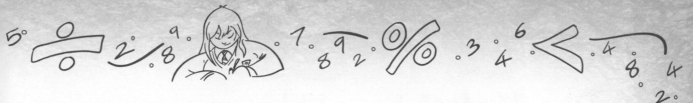

FURTHER PRACTICE

75.**8** × 4.**2**

$$
\begin{array}{r}
75.8 \\
4.2 \times \\
\hline
1\,5^11^16 \\
3\,0^23^32\,0 \\
\hline
3\,1\,8.\mathbf{3\,6}
\end{array}
$$

There is a total of two decimal places in the question (the 2 and the 8) so there must be two decimal places in the answer.

Estimate your answer:

75.8 × 4.2 ≈ 80 × 4 = 320.

So 318.36 seems a reasonable answer.

EXAMINER'S TOP TIPS

- For +, − and ÷ set out your working so the decimals are aligned above each other.

- For × it's easiest to ignore decimals until the end. The number of decimals in total in the question will be the same as the number you need in the answer.

- Use a method of working that is quick and accurate.

- Your working must be clear, so that the examiner can see how you reached your answer.

- Forgetting the 0s when multiplying is a very common error.

- Estimate the answer in your head at the beginning. Your calculated answer shouldn't be too different.

Predictable patterns

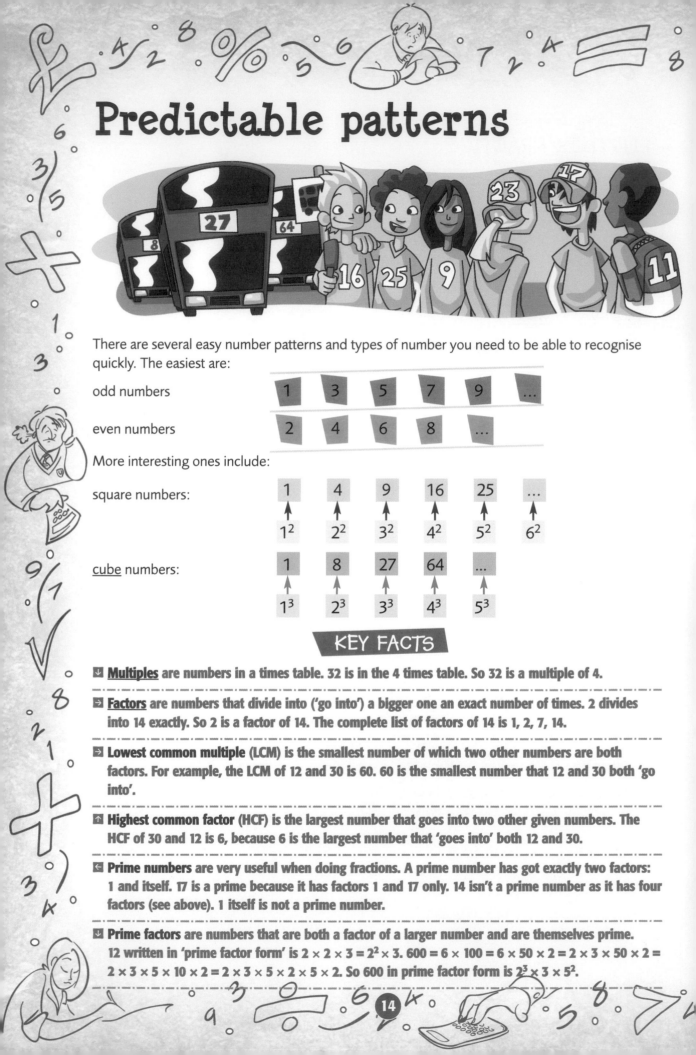

There are several easy number patterns and types of number you need to be able to recognise quickly. The easiest are:

odd numbers

| 1 | 3 | 5 | 7 | 9 | ... |

even numbers

| 2 | 4 | 6 | 8 | ... |

More interesting ones include:

square numbers:

| 1 | 4 | 9 | 16 | 25 | ... |

1^2 2^2 3^2 4^2 5^2 6^2

cube numbers:

| 1 | 8 | 27 | 64 | ... |

1^3 2^3 3^3 4^3 5^3

KEY FACTS

↳ **Multiples** are numbers in a times table. 32 is in the 4 times table. So 32 is a multiple of 4.

➔ **Factors** are numbers that divide into ('go into') a bigger one an exact number of times. 2 divides into 14 exactly. So 2 is a factor of 14. The complete list of factors of 14 is 1, 2, 7, 14.

➔ **Lowest common multiple (LCM)** is the smallest number of which two other numbers are both factors. For example, the LCM of 12 and 30 is 60. 60 is the smallest number that 12 and 30 both 'go into'.

↥ **Highest common factor (HCF)** is the largest number that goes into two other given numbers. The HCF of 30 and 12 is 6, because 6 is the largest number that 'goes into' both 12 and 30.

↰ **Prime numbers** are very useful when doing fractions. A prime number has got exactly two factors: 1 and itself. 17 is a prime because it has factors 1 and 17 only. 14 isn't a prime number as it has four factors (see above). 1 itself is not a prime number.

↴ **Prime factors** are numbers that are both a factor of a larger number and are themselves prime. 12 written in 'prime factor form' is $2 \times 2 \times 3 = 2^2 \times 3$. $600 = 6 \times 100 = 6 \times 50 \times 2 = 2 \times 3 \times 50 \times 2 = 2 \times 3 \times 5 \times 10 \times 2 = 2 \times 3 \times 5 \times 2 \times 5 \times 2$. So 600 in prime factor form is $2^3 \times 3 \times 5^2$.

FURTHER PRACTICE

The following numbers have been rewritten in prime factor form:

a) $60 = 6 \times 10 = 2 \times 3 \times 5 \times 2 = 2^2 \times 3 \times 5$

b) $45 = 5 \times 9 = 5 \times 3 \times 3 = 3^2 \times 5$

c) $56 = 7 \times 8 = 7 \times 2 \times 2 \times 2 = 2^3 \times 7$

Now answer the following questions.

1 Which of the numbers below are:

a) cube numbers

b) square numbers

c) multiples of 4

d) factors of 660

e) prime numbers?

21	22	23	24	25	26	27	28	29	30

2 Find:

a) the lowest common multiple of 32 and 80

b) the highest common factor of 32 and 80.

EXAMINER'S TOP TIPS

When writing out a number in prime factor form don't forget to write the final answer as a <u>product</u> (multiplication), e.g. $2^3 \times 7$.

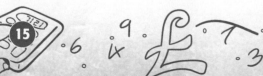
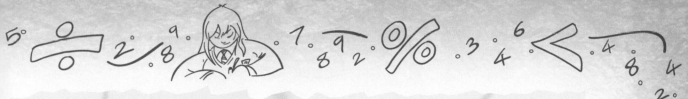

Ratty ratios

A nature programme on TV is exploring the family life of rats. It explains that there are so many that we all live within a few feet of a rat.

The ratio of adult rats to young rats in a population is 2:5. So if there are 250 adult rats, how many young rats are there?

Working out ratios is fairly simple, but there are two main types to look out for. Which type depends on what you're told.

1   Here you know about one part of the ratio, the **adults**.

The ratio is **2:5**.

So, 250 (adult rats) ≡ **2** parts.
(≡ means equivalent to)

You can now work out how many rats 1 part is:

1 part ≡ 250 ÷ 2 ≡ 125 rats.

The young rats have **5** parts of the ratio, which means:

5 × 125 ≡ 625 young rats.

2   Alternatively you might be told there are 420 rats **altogether**. If the ratio of adult rats to young rats is 2:5, how many adults are there, and how many young?

Using the same ratio of 2:5 means there are 7 parts in the ratio **in total**.

7 parts ≡ 420 rats

So 1 part ≡ 420 ÷ 7 = 60 rats

Using the ratio there are:

2 × 60 adults : 5 × 60 young

≡ 120 adults and 300 young

Other types of ratio question involve simplifying, e.g.:

Simplify the ratio 8:20.

Dividing by 2 gives 4:10.

Dividing by 2 again gives 2:5.

So 2:5 is equivalent to 8:20.

FURTHER PRACTICE

1 Simplify the following ratios as far as possible:

a) 4:12

b) 12:42

c) 2:8:26

2 The three ratios below are equivalent. Find x and y.

3:5 x:105   27:y

3 The ratio of sale price to profit for a company's products is 9:2.

If the company sells a product for £72 how much profit does it make?

4 Jane, Clare and Sarah are going to share a £450 lottery win in the ratio of their ages. Jane is half Clare's age. Sarah is three times Clare's age. How much should each girl receive?

Answers

1 a 1:3
   b 2:7
   c 1:4:13

2 x = (105 ÷ 5) × 3 = 63, y = (27 ÷ 3) × 5 = 45

3 9 parts = £72, 1 part = £8, profit = 2 parts = 2 × £8 = £16

4 One valid ratio for ages Jane:Clare:Sarah is 1:2:6
   Total 9 parts = £450, so 1 part = 450 ÷ 9 = £50
   Jane = 1 × £50 = £50
   Clare = 2 × £50 = £100
   Sarah = 6 × £50 = £300
   Check: total = 50 + 100 + 300 = £450 ✓

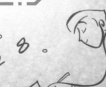

×/÷ OPERATIONS

$$\oplus \times \oplus = \oplus \qquad \oplus \div \oplus = \oplus$$
$$\oplus \times \ominus = \ominus \qquad \oplus \div \ominus = \ominus$$
$$\ominus \times \oplus = \ominus \qquad \ominus \div \oplus = \ominus$$
$$\ominus \times \ominus = \oplus \qquad \ominus \div \ominus = \oplus$$

ALSO
WORK
FOR PLUS
MINUS
SIDE BY
SIDE
eg.
$5 + -3 = 5$
$ - 3$
$ = 2$

+/− O
There is
rule, it's size
of number th
matters.

NUM

PATTERNS

1, 4, 9, 16 Square Numbers
1, 3, 6, 9, 10 Triangle Numbers

FRACTIONS

+/− Common denominator

eg. $\dfrac{1}{2} + \dfrac{3}{4} = \dfrac{2}{4} + \dfrac{3}{4} = \dfrac{5}{4} = 1\dfrac{1}{4}$

$\dfrac{2}{3} \times 12 = \dfrac{2}{3} \times \dfrac{12}{1} = \dfrac{24}{3} = 8$

TO
$\dfrac{3}{4} = 3$

OVER 10
e.g. 0.4
e.g. 0.32 =

TURN INTO DECIMAL FIRST

OVER 100 CANCEL DOWN
eg. 12% = $\dfrac{12}{100} = \dfrac{6}{50} = \dfrac{3}{25}$

× 10, × 100 ÷ 10 etc
×
decimal appears to move to the
right or number appears to move
to the left
÷
decimal appears to move to the
left or number appears to move
to the right
$2.683 \times 100 = 268.3$
$32.5 \div 10 = 3.25$
$0.032 \div 100 = 0.00032$

PERCE

12% of 45 =
15 out of 60 = $\dfrac{15}{6}$

TIONS

5+3=-2

+5=+2

3:2

4:2

3:4

3:5

6:5

RATIO

6:2 → 3:1

£40 split 3:1 → £30 : £10

BERS

MULTIPLES / FACTORS

eg. 4 is a Factor of 12

20 is a multiple of 5

3 is a prime Factor of 15

4.62

TOM

.75

.7

DECIMALS

Rounding

4.58 = 5 (nearest whole no.)

= **4.6** (1 decimal place)

0.181818 ... = $0.\dot{1}\dot{8}$

0.99999 ... = $0.\dot{9}$

$\frac{2}{5}$

$\frac{6}{0} = \frac{8}{25}$

0%

ES

$45 = 0.12 \times 45 = 5.4$

$\times 100 = \frac{1}{4} \times 100 = 25\%$

+100

TURN INTO FRACTION FIRST

PRIME NUMBERS

Have exactly 2 factors,

eg. 2, 3, 5, 7, 11, 13 etc.

6 is NOT prime

its factors are 1, 2, 3, 6

75.7

LOWEST COMMON MULTIPLE

LCM of 6 and 8

Multiples of 6

6, 12, 18, 24 , 3 ...

Multiples of 8

8, 16, 24 , 32 ...

Lowest number that 6 and 8 are both factors of is 24.

7%

19

Test your knowledge 1

X means non-calculator questions.

X **1** Calculate each of the following. Give your answers as fractions in their simplest form.

    a) $\frac{3}{4} \times \frac{5}{12}$ [1]

    b) $\frac{3}{4} + \frac{5}{12}$ [1]

    c) $\frac{3}{4} \div \frac{5}{12}$ [1]

    d) $\frac{3}{4} - \frac{2}{5}$ [1]

X **2** a) Increase 680 kg by 23%. [1]

    b) Decrease £234 by 24%. [1]

    c) Increase $203 by 3%. [1]

    d) Decrease 346 g by 30%. [1]

X **3** a) $3 + (4 \div 2)$ [1]

    b) $(3 + 4) \div 2$ [1]

    c) $(5 + 3) \div 2^2 + 1$ [1]

    d) $4(3 + 1) - 2$ [1]

X **4** Approximate the answers to the following calculations:

    a) 317×491 [1]

    b) $1555 - 1492$ [1]

    c) $125.3 \div 24.9$ [1]

    d) $1.82 + 14.82$ [1]

X **5** a) List all the prime numbers between 20 and 35. [1]

    b) Write down a square number which is also a cube number. [1]

    c) Write 48 in prime factor form. [1]

    d) Find the lowest common multiple of 48 and 50. [1]

6 Calculate the following, showing all your working:

    a) $12.89 + 5.13$ **[1]**

    b) $89.92 - 3.69$ **[1]**

    c) 5.2×16.38 **[1]**

    d) $132.05 \div 5$ **[1]**

7 a) £343 is to be shared between two brothers in the ratio 3:4.
      How much will each brother receive?   **[2]**

    b) Two sisters share a gift from their aunt. The ratio of money
      received by sister A to that received by sister B is 3:4.
      If sister A receives £345, how much does sister B receive?   **[2]**

8 £2000 is placed in a building society account. Interest is added
at 5% per year. No further deposits or withdrawals are made.
How much is in the account three years later?   **[2]**

9 The price of a product is increased by 10%. This new price is later reduced by 10%.
Explain why the price of the product does not return to its original value.   **[2]**

10 Cancel these fractions to their simplest form.

    a) $\dfrac{21}{49}$ **[1]**

    b) $\dfrac{35}{49}$ **[1]**

    c) $\dfrac{60}{98}$ **[1]**

11 a) Express $\dfrac{2}{5}$ as a decimal.   **[1]**

    b) Express $\dfrac{2}{5}$ as a percentage.   **[1]**

    c) Find $\dfrac{2}{5}$ of 160 kg.   **[1]**

(Total 38 marks)

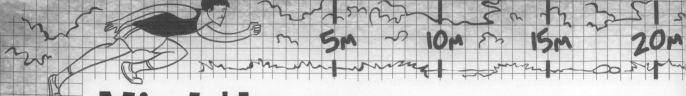
Mind the gap

Class 9W is doing a biology project on pond life. Today they are studying the movements of the largest frog in the pond.

The frog leaps 15 cm with each hop. It starts on dry land, 10 cm away from the edge of the school pond. It hops away from the pond in a straight line.

The numbers below are the distances (in cm) of the frog from the pond each time it lands.

10, 25, 40, 55, 70, 85…

A list of numbers with a set pattern like this is called a <u>sequence</u>. When studying sequences, you use '**n**' to represent the position of any number in the sequence. For example:

The **2**nd number in the sequence is **25**. So when **n = 2,** the distance is **25 cm**.
The **4**th number in the sequence is **55**. So when **n = 4**, the distance is **55 cm**.

Here is a table showing the first six numbers in the sequence:

n	1	2	3	4	5	6
d	10	25	40	55	70	85

There is a quick rule to work out the pattern number (d) for any value of n. You need to work out the difference between each distance. There is always a gap of 15 – Froggie's hop distance.

Pick a value of n, say **n = 3**. Multiply this by 15 and you get 45. The distance for $n = 3$ is actually 40. So you would have to subtract 5 from your answer to get the distance.

Your quick way to find the distance is now clear:

Multiply n by 15, and then subtract 5.
So: $d = 15n - 5$

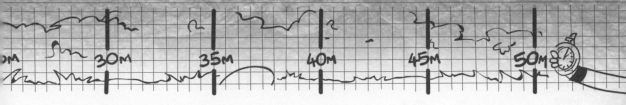

FURTHER PRACTICE

Look at the working below, then try the four questions yourself.

8, 13, 18, 23, 28 The gap is always 5.

When n = 4 pattern number is 20. 5 × 4 = 20.

The actual distance is 23 so add 3.

Expression is $5n + 3$.

Check for n = 2:

$5n + 3 = 5(2) + 3 = 10 + 3 = 13.$ ✓

1 99, 114, 129, 144, 159

2 50, 58, 66, 74, 82

3 −2, 1, 4, 7, 10

4 16, 14, 12, 10, 8

EXAMINER'S TOP TIPS

You don't have to check that your expression works, but it is really sensible to do so. Any value of n will do. Look how the answers (below) have been checked.

You can use any letter you like. It doesn't have to be 'n' all the time.

KEY FACTS

⬇ **You multiply the position number (n) by the gap.**

➡ **Then adjust this number by trying a value out.**

Answers

1 Gap = 15. For n = 4, $15n$ = 15 × 4 = 60. You wanted 144, so add 84. So expression is $15n + 84$.
Check: For n = 3, $15n$ + 84 = 15(3) + 84 = 45 + 84 = 129 ✓

2 Gap = 8. For n = 3, $8n$ = 8 × 3 = 24. You wanted 66, so add 42. So expression is $8n + 42$.
Check: For n = 4, $8n$ + 42 = 8(4) + 42 = 32 + 42 = 74 ✓

3 Gap = 3. For n = 2, $3n$ = 3 × 2 = 6. You wanted 1, so subtract 5. So expression is $3n - 5$.
Check: For n = 4, $3n - 5 = 3(4) - 5 = 12 - 5 = 7$ ✓

4 Gap = −2. For n = 3, $-2n = -2 × 3 = -6$. You wanted 12, so add 18. So expression is $-2n + 18$.
Check: For n = 2, $-2n + 18 = -2(2) + 18 = -4 + 18 = 14$ ✓

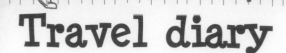

Travel diary

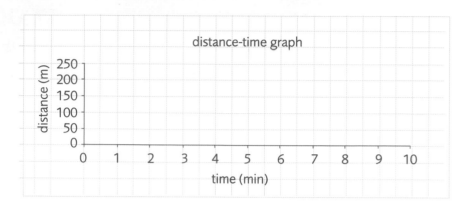

distance-time graph

Here's a typical distance–time graph, but can you work out whose journey it shows?

a) This man is driving his miniature train to the end of his garden and then reversing it back.

b) This girl is chatting on her mobile as she walks around the park, getting slower and slower.

The answer is (a) but how do you know?

The distance–time graph shows several pieces of information:

c) This dog is snoozing in the sun before leaping up and chasing a ball.

- The straight line from (0,0) to (2,200) shows that the train starts off at a constant <u>speed</u>. The speed is $\frac{200\,m}{120\,sec} = 1\frac{2}{3}\,m/s$.

- Point (2,200) shows that the end of the garden is 200 m away and it takes 2 minutes to reach it.

- The horizontal part is where the train is not moving. It is stationary at the end of the garden for 3 minutes.

- The slope in the third part of the journey is half of that in the first part. This shows that the train returns at half the previous speed.

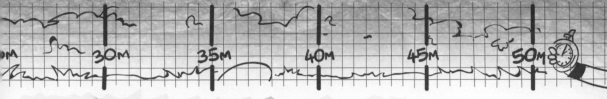

FURTHER PRACTICE

Try the questions below. Check each answer (see bottom of the page) and make sure that you understand them.

1 The distance–time graph below shows the journeys for three sprinters training together to run the 100 m. Describe fully the practice race shown by the graph.

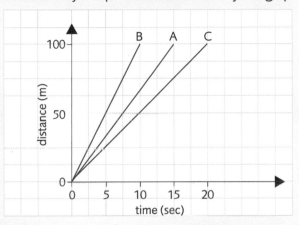

2 Darren runs to the corner shop to buy a newspaper. A distance–time graph for the journey is shown below.

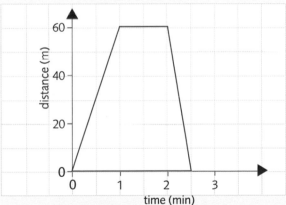

a) How far away is the corner shop?

b) How fast did Darren run on the way to and from the shop in metres per second?

c) How long was Darren in the shop?

EXAMINER'S TOP TIPS

Take care to look at the units used on the axes. You may need to change them, as in question 2b) below.

KEY FACTS

In distance–time graphs:

↓ a straight line means constant speed

→ a horizontal line means no speed

↑ $speed = \dfrac{change\ in\ distance}{time\ taken}$

$S = \dfrac{D}{T}$

Answers

1 Each runner travels at a constant speed, as the lines are straight. Runner B is first, followed by runners A and C. The runners' speeds are 10 m/s, $6\frac{2}{3}$ m/s and 5 m/s.

2a) 60 m

2b) 1 min = 60 sec. To the shop, speed $= \frac{60\,m}{60\,sec} = 1$ m/s. Return speed $= \frac{60\,m}{30\,sec} = 2$ m/s.

2c) 1 minute

105

Take care to look at the units

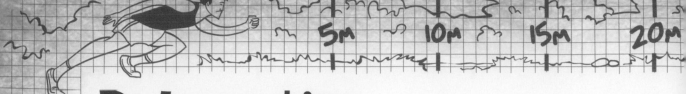
Redecorating

Anastasia is redecorating her bedroom. It's a huge job, and she doesn't fancy stripping the wallpaper off before painting the walls.

To make it easier she hires a wallpaper stripper from her local hardware store. There's a fixed cost of £6 to hire the machine plus £5 for each day that she has it.

A few days later the store sends her a bill for £41. How many days has Anastasia had the machine?

In questions like this it helps to <u>form an equation</u> which you can then <u>solve</u>. If d is the number of days that Anastasia had the machine, and remembering that each of these days cost £5, then the equation to solve is:

$$5d + 6 = 41$$

One way to work it out is to imagine how the store arrived at the total cost of £41. They took d, multiplied it by 5 and then added 6, getting 41. If you write this out as a flowchart and then work through it in reverse, you can solve the problem.

(You must follow the rules of BIDMAS, though: see pages 8–9.)

$$d \rightarrow \times 5 \rightarrow + 6 \rightarrow 41$$

$$d \leftarrow \div 5 \leftarrow - 6 \leftarrow 41$$

Starting from the right:

$$d = 41 - 6 = 35$$
$$35 \div 5 = 7$$
$$\text{So } d = 7$$

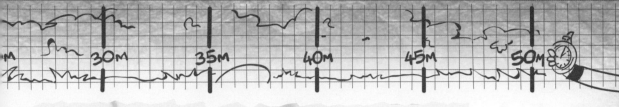

FURTHER PRACTICE

Can you solve each of these questions? Use any method you like – the answers are at the bottom of the page.

1 $6e - 4 = 2$

2 $2(x + 3) = 14$

3 $3n^2 + 1 = 49$

4 $2(a - 1)^2 = 50$

5   A rectangle's length is four times its width. Its perimeter is 35 m. Find its area.

KEY FACTS

☑ The important part of 'reading' an equation is imagining what the numbers in the equation are doing to the letter, and in what order.

☑ In $5d + 6$ the first thing that changes the d value is that it is multiplied by 5, then + 6. This determines the order of the flowchart boxes.

☑ To unravel the equation, you simply have to follow the flowchart in reverse.

EXAMINER'S TOP TIPS

When you think you've got the answer, put it back into the equation and see if it works.

In question 1, if you think $e = 2$, put 2 into the equation. $(6 \times 2) - 4$ actually equals 8, not 2, so you know you've made a mistake!

Answers

1   $e = 1$. Working: $(2 + 4) \div 6$
2   $x = 4$. Working: $(14 \div 2) - 3 = 4$
3   $n = \pm 4$. Working: $(49 - 1) \div 3 = 16$. Square root of 16 = plus or minus 4.
4   $a = -4$ or 6. Working: $(50 \div 2) = 25$. Square root of 25 = plus or minus 5. $-5 + 1 = -4$. $5 + 1 = 6$
5   $A = 49 \text{ m}^2$. Working: $4w + w + 4w + w = 35$. $10w = 35$. $w = 3.5$. $4w = 4 \times 3.5 = 14 \text{ m}$. $A = \text{base} \times \text{height} = 14 \times 3.5 = 49 \text{ m}^2$.

Pets' corner

Yasmin is doing a DT project at school which involves building a garden playpen for a puppy. Two sides of the playpen will be garden walls and the other two sides will be made of fencing. She is told that the fencing must total 10 m in length, and that the playpen must enclose an area of 12 m².

She needs to work out what the dimensions of the playpen are to the nearest 10 cm. The area of a rectangle is found by multiplying the base by the height. Taking the base as w, and the height as $10 - w$ (as the fencing is 10 m long in total), she writes:

$$\text{Area} = w(10 - w) = 10w - w^2.$$

To solve $10w - w^2 = 12$, Yasmin needs a calculator and some patience. The method she uses is called 'trial and improvement'. It works like this:

She tries:	$10w - w^2$	She decides:
$w = 2$	$20 - 2^2 = 16$	too high (H) – she wants 12 not 16
$w = 1$	$10 - 1^2 = 9$	too low (L)
$w = 1.5$	$15 - 1.5^2 = 12.75$	(H)
$w = 1.4$	$14 - 1.4^2 = 12.04$	(H) – close though!
$w = 1.3$	$13 - 1.3^2 = 11.31$	(L) 1.4 seems nearer

So w is between 1.3 and 1.4. To be certain which is nearer, she tries $w = 1.35$.

$w = 1.35$	$13.5 - 1.35^2 = 11.67$	(L)

Since 11.67 is too low, it's clear the value of w is between 1.35 and 1.4. So it has to round to 1.4.

So $w = 1.4$ m (2sf)

And the other dimension is:

$$10 - w = 10 - 1.4 = 8.6 \, \text{m}.$$

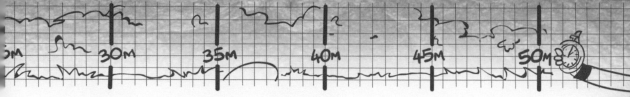

FURTHER PRACTICE

Using trial and improvement, solve $t^3 = 30$ to 1dp. Look at each line of working carefully. Can you follow the logic of the values of t used at each stage?

Try $t = 3$	$3^3 = 27$	(L)
Try $t = 4$	$4^3 = 64$	(H) – very high, 3 much closer
Try $t = 3.2$	$3.2^3 = 32.768$	(H)
Try $t = 3.1$	$3.1^3 = 29.791$	(L) – between 3.1 and 3.2
Try $t = 3.15$	$3.15^3 = 31.25...$	(H)

So t is between 3.1 and 3.15. Whatever the number's second decimal place, t will round down to 3.1.

$$t = 3.1 \text{ (1dp)}$$

Now try this one yourself. The first line has been done for you: can you complete the working? Check your answer below when you're finished.

Solve $n^2 - 9n + 10 = 0$ to 2dp using $n = 6$ as a first estimate.

$$n = 6 \qquad 6^2 - 9(6) + 10 = 36 - 54 + 10 = -8 \text{ (L)}$$

KEY FACTS

- When solving an equation using trial and improvement you simply substitute numbers into the equation until the number you use is sufficiently accurate. The next number you choose depends on how well your last choice worked.

- To get your answer to any required accuracy, you'll need to try one value that has one more decimal place than your final answer. In the example above the last attempt was 3.15 (i.e. to 2dp). This leads you to the final answer of 3.1 (1dp).

EXAMINER'S TOP TIPS

Lots of people lose marks because they do everything except write down the final answer. In the example above they put '31.3 (31.25 to 1dp)' rather than the correct answer, '$t = 3.1$'. It's t (or n, or w etc.) that the examiner wants to see!

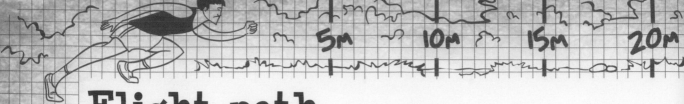

Flight path

At an airport, Air Traffic Control has to advise the pilot about the best flight path for landing.

Assuming the flight path is a straight line, the plane might descend from a height of 2 km (about 6000 ft) over a horizontal distance of 10 km. A graph of the descent would look like this:

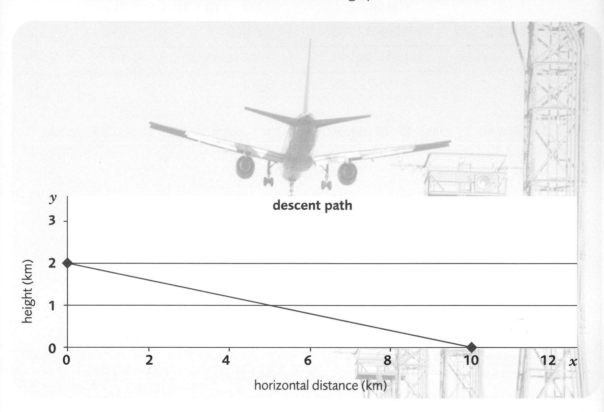

- The slope is called the gradient, *m*. *m* = increase in height ÷ horizontal distance (up ÷ along).

- On the line, *x* is the horizontal distance, and *y* is the height.

- The point where the line cuts the *y* axis (height) is called the intercept, *c*.

The equation of a generally straight line is $y = mx + c$.

For this aeroplane: $m = \frac{-2}{10} = \frac{-1}{5}$, and $c = 2$.

The equation of the line is therefore $y = \frac{-1}{5}x + 2$.

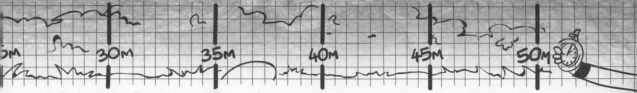

FURTHER PRACTICE

Make sure you understand how the answers to these questions are worked out.

1 Find the equations of each line on the graph.

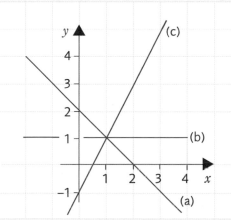

a) $c = 2$, $m = \frac{-2}{2} = -1$.　　Answer: $y = -x + 2$

b) y is always 1 along this line.

　　　　　　　　　　　　Answer: $y = 1$

c) $c = -1$, $m = \frac{4}{2} = 2$.　　Answer: $y = 2x - 1$

2 Sketch the lines described by the equations given:

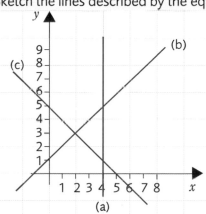

a) $x = 4$

b) $y = x + 1$

c) $y = 5 - x$

For $x = 4$, x is always 4. This is therefore a line parallel to the y axis.

For $y = x + 1$, both the intercept (c) and gradient (m) are 1.

For $y = 5 - x$, it's best to write this as $y = -x + 5$ first. This is therefore a line with intercept 5 and gradient -1.

The equation of a straight line is:

$$y = mx + c$$

number on the y axis (vertical)	gradient (up/along)	number on the x axis (horizontal)	the y intercept – where the line cuts the y axis

EXAMINER'S TOP TIPS

It's easy to get the simplest of lines muddled up. For example, $y = 4$ is parallel to the x axis, not to the y axis as so many people think.

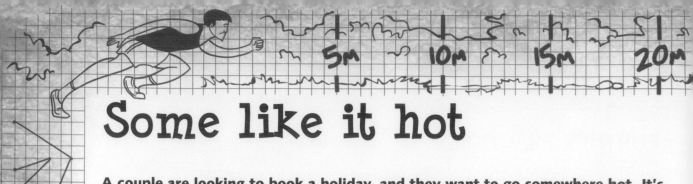

Some like it hot

A couple are looking to book a holiday, and they want to go somewhere hot. It's 29°C in Tenerife, and they want to know what that is in Fahrenheit, to see whether it's worth booking a flight.

An equation for converting temperatures from degrees Centigrade (°C) into degrees Fahrenheit (°F) is:

$$F = 1.8C + 32$$

All they need to do is to <u>substitute</u> numbers into the equation:

C = 29, so

$$F = 1.8 \times 29 + 32 = 52.2 + 32 = 84.2 = 84°F$$

In this form the equation $F = 1.8C + 32$ is similar to $y = mx + c$.
Plot a graph of F against C and think about the gradient and intercept (see pages 30–31.)

So 29°C is about 84°F, and they book their flight immediately.

What would C be if F = 212°F?

212 = 1.8C + 32
212 – 32 = 1.8C
180 = 1.8C
C = 180 ÷ 1.8 = 100°C
So 212°F = 100°C (the boiling point of water)

(Note that sometimes there are more than two letters in the equation.)

To fill in a table of values you will have to substitute several times into the same equation. This table is for the equation above:

C	0	25	50	75	100
F	32	77	122	167	212

$F = 1.8 \times 75 + 32$

You can then use the table to plot the graph of the equation:

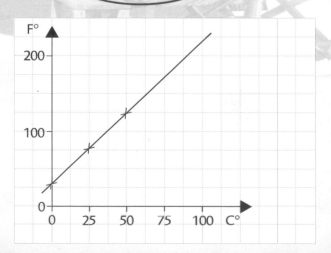

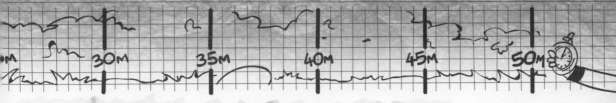

FURTHER PRACTICE

Here is the start of a table of values for the equation $y = 2x + 1$.

x	–2	–1	0	1	2
y					

Look at how it has been completed:

$2(2) + 1 = 4 + 1 = 5$

x	–2	**–1**	0	1	**2**
y	–3	–1	1	3	5

$2(-1) + 1 = -2 + 1 = -1$

EXAMINER'S TOP TIPS

When filling in a values table, start with the right-hand numbers. These are usually positive and therefore easier!

Now try these questions on your own:

1 Given that $L = 2(a + b)$ find L when:

a) $a = 3$, $b = 5$

b) $a = -2$, $b = -3$

c) $a = b = 6$

2 The surface area, S, of a cuboid with side l is given by the equation $S = 6l^2$. Given that l is 10 cm, find S.

3 Pythagoras' theorem states that, in a right-angled triangle, the sides are related by the equation $a^2 + b^2 = c^2$, where c is the length of the side opposite the right angle.

a) If $a = 5$ and $b = 12$, find c.

b) If $a = 9$ and $c = 15$, find b.

KEY FACTS

☑ **Substitute means to replace letters with numbers in an equation.**

➡ **Use BIDMAS to help you do this (see pages 8–9).**

Answers

1 a) $L = 2(3 + 5) = 16$
b) $L = 2(-2 + -3) = -10$
c) $2(6 + 6) = 24$
2 $6 \times 10^2 = 6 \times 100 = 600 \, cm^2$
3 a) $5^2 + 12^2 = c^2$
$25 + 144 = c^2$
$169 = c^2$
$c = 13$
b) $9^2 + b^2 = 15^2$
$81 + b^2 = 225$
$b^2 = 225 - 81 = 144$
$b = 12$

Text or call?

A new mobile phone company offers several tariff options. One tariff allows you to choose a certain number of free texts or free calls each month. The phone company designs an equation connecting the number of free texts (T) to the number of free minutes (M) of calls:

$$4M + T = 240$$

You need to draw a graph to help you decide what combination of free texts and calls you want to choose.

When you have an equation like this to plot, it is easiest to find where the graph meets the two axes first. Put M = 0 and work out T, and then put T = 0 and work out M.

M = 0: 4(0) + T = 240. So T = 240.

T = 0: 4M + 0 = 240. So M = 60.

You can now plot these two points (0, 240) and (60, 0) on the axes:

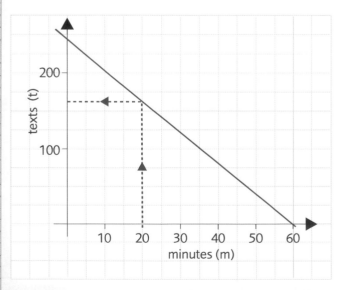

Finding other points on the line is simple. How many free texts would you have on this tariff if you chose to have 20 minutes of free calls?

M = 20
4M + T = 240
4(20) + T = 240
80 + T = 240
So T = 160, i.e. 160 free texts.

You can also read the answer from the graph. You need to know how to use both methods.

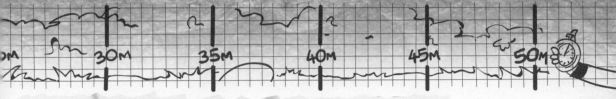

FURTHER PRACTICE

1 A line has equation $2x + 3y = 12$.

a) When $x = 3$, find y.

b) Sketch the graph of the line.

2 a) Sketch the graph of the line $p + q = 4$ on the axes provided.

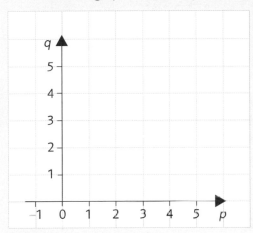

b) When $p = 3$, find q.

c) when $q = 1$, find p.

EXAMINER'S TOP TIPS

Be careful which way round the axes are if they're not the common x and y ones.

KEY FACTS

⬇ The graph of an equation such as $2x + 3y = 12$ is a straight line.

➡ Putting $x = 0$ and $y = 0$ finds the points where it meets the y and x axes.

⬇ Plot these two points and join them together with a straight line to make your graph.

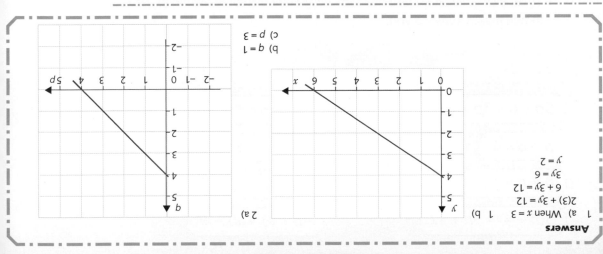

Answers

1 a) When $x = 3$ 1 b)
$2(3) + 3y = 12$
$6 + 3y = 12$
$3y = 6$
$y = 2$

2 a)

b) $q = 1$
c) $p = 3$

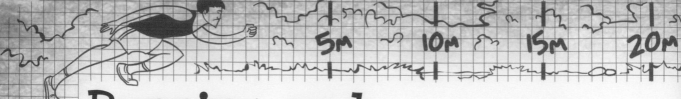

Running mad

A documentary on TV features three marathon runners, Carol, David and Jason. Between them they have 134 years' experience of running marathons.

Carol has been running marathons for six years longer than David.
Jason has been running marathons twice as long as David.
How long has each of them been running marathons?

You can tackle this sort of problem with a little bit of algebra.

- Start with David's years, as he's been running for the shortest time. Call David's years y.

- So Carol's would be $y + 6$ and Jason would be $2y$.

- You can now form an <u>equation</u> for their total number of years marathon running:

$$y + y + 6 + 2y = 134$$

- You can <u>simplify</u> this equation:

$$4y + 6 = 134$$
$$4y = 134 - 6$$
$$4y = 128$$
$$y = 128 \div 4 = 32 \text{ years}$$

So David = 32 years, Carol = 32 + 6 = 38 years, and Jason = 2 × 32 = 64 years.

There are several simplifications you need to know. Here are some examples.
Check each one makes sense to you.

$3x + 2x - x = 4x$	$\dfrac{12q}{4q} = 3$
$5p + 6 - 3p + 1 = 2p + 7$	$24t^3 \div 6 = 4t^3$
$p \div p = 1$	$3y^2 \times 2y = 6y^3$
$n \times n = n^2$	$2p^2 + 3p^2 = 5p^2$
$3(n + 4) = 3n + 12$	$a(b - a) = ab - a^2$

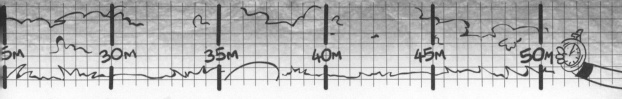

FURTHER PRACTICE

1 Simplify each of the following:

a) $2w + 5 + 3w - 7$

b) $5q - 3t - 2q - 3t$

c) $x^2 - 2xy + 2x^2 + 3xy$

2 Simplify these expressions as far as possible:

a) $m(n + 3) + m(2 + n)$

b) $6(p - 2q) + 4(2p + 3q)$

3 When asked to simplify the expression $\frac{1}{x} + \frac{1}{y}$, a pupil wrote $\frac{2}{(x + y)}$.
Find values for x and y which show this to be wrong.

EXAMINER'S TOP TIPS

You need to be familiar with several different ways of simplifying equations. Reread the box at the bottom of page 36.

Sometimes people don't simplify far enough. In question 2b above, there are two different steps in getting the final answer. Always look for more than one.

KEY FACTS

⬇ Simplifying is a way of making algebraic expressions less complicated. The shorter and simpler they are, the easier they are to read and understand. If the expression is part of an equation, it will be easier to solve or use if expressions within it have been simplified first.

Answers

1 a) $5w - 2$
   b) $3q - 6t$
   c) $3x^2 + xy$
2 a) $mn + 3m + 2m + mn = 2mn + 5m$
   b) $6p - 12q + 8p + 12q = 14p$
3 Choose any values for x and y. Let $x = y = 2$
   $\frac{1}{x} + \frac{1}{y} = \frac{1}{2} + \frac{1}{2} = 1$ But $\frac{2}{(x+y)} = \frac{2}{(2+2)} = \frac{2}{4} = \frac{1}{2}$. Clearly $\frac{1}{2} \neq 1$.

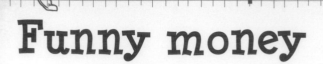

Funny money

Greg is off to France on a school canoeing trip. He has £50 spending money.

The exchange rate is £1 ≡ 1.45€.

How many euros can Greg take to France?

$$£1 ≡ 1.45€$$
$$£50 ≡ 50 × 1.45 = 72.50€$$

Greg comes back with 12€. How much is this worth in sterling (£)?

$$£1 ≡ 1.45€$$
$$\text{So } 1€ ≡ £(1 ÷ 1.45)$$
$$\text{So } 12€ ≡ £12 × (1 ÷ 1.45)$$
$$= \frac{£12}{1.45} = £8.28$$

Notice that in doing one conversion Greg has to multiply by 1.45, and in the other he has to divide by 1.45. Obviously he needs to be careful which one he chooses.

The canoe instructor told the group that they had canoed a total of 28 km during the week. 8 km ≡ 5 miles. To work out how far this is in miles is easy.

If 8 km ≡ 5 miles, then miles are longer than kilometres, and 1 km ≡ $\frac{5}{8}$ mile.

So 28 km ≡ 28 × $\left(\frac{5}{8}\right)$ mile ≡ 28 × 5 ÷ 8 ≡ 140 ÷ 8 ≡ 17.5 miles.

To convert from miles to km, instead of × $\frac{5}{8}$ you would × $\frac{8}{5}$.

Some people think of × $\frac{8}{5}$ as × 1.6, and × $\frac{5}{8}$ as ÷ 1.6.

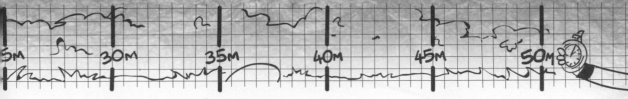

FURTHER PRACTICE

Check how these sums are worked out, then fill in the missing answers.

You will need the currency convertion rates (below) in these questions.

1 Convert £250 into each currency:

a) US$: 250 × 1.91 ≡ $477.50

b) Euros: 250 × 1.452 ≡ €363.00

c) Yen:

> £1 ≡ US$1.91
> ≡ €1.452
> ≡ Y201.80

2 Convert each amount of currency into £s:

a) €500:   500 ÷ 1.452 = £344.35

b) Y100,000:   100,000 ÷ 201.8 ≡ £495.54

c) US$500:

3 A farmer reckons that a fit sheepdog can run up to 100 km per day whilst being worked by a shepherd on the cliffs of Cornwall. Calculate how far such a sheepdog is thought to run in miles per day.

KEY FACTS

↷ **An easy way to think of converting from one currency to another is to either × or ÷ by the exchange rate.**

EXAMINER'S TOP TIPS

Don't forget to give the units with your answer.

The examiner needs to know if your answer is £, miles, litres etc.

B - Brackets
I - Indices
D - Division
M - Multiplication
A - Addition
S - Subtraction

EXPRESSIONS

don't have = signs
e.g. 3a + b, xy

Follow the arrows to

ALG

SIMPLIFICATION

$ab + bc = b(a + c)$

$x \times x = x^2 \quad a^2\, a^3 = a^5$

$\dfrac{6a}{3} = 2a \qquad \dfrac{a^3}{a} = a^2$

$3 \times a = 3a$

$a + a = 2a \qquad 3p + 2p = 5p$

$6p^2 - 4p^2 = 2p^2$

SEQUENCES
(patterns)

TERM TO TERM

e.g. 5, 9, 13, 17, 21
    + 4   + 4

PREDICTION

Next term = 21 + 4 = 25

POSITION TO TERM

n	1	2	3	4	5	Position
p	5	9	13	17	21	Term

+4

Gap = 4   So try p = 4n
pick n = 3 (or any other)
p = 4n = 4 (3) = 12
But for n = 3, p = 13
So you need to add 1

∴ P = 4n + 1

GRAPHICAL FORM

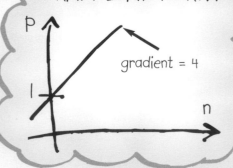

gradient = 4

SUBSTITUTION

If $a = 2$ $b = 3$ $c = -4$
Find ab, bc, c^2, c/a
$ab = 2 \times 3 = 6$
$bc = 3 \times -4 = -12$
$c^2 = -4 \times -4 = 16$
$c/a = -4 \div 2 = -2$

TRIAL AND IMPROVEMENT

repeated substitution
SOLVE $x^2 + 3x - 2 = 0$
Try $x = 1$: $1^2 + 3(1) - 2 = 2$ (H)
Try $x = 0$: $0^2 + 3(0) - 2 = -2$ (L)
$x = 0.5$: $0.5^2 + 3(0.5) - 2 = -\frac{1}{4}$ (L)
$x = 0.6$: $0.6^2 + 3(0.6) - 2 = 0.16$ (H)
$x = 0.55 \dots$

explore types of algebra

EBRA

$Y = 3A + B$

$X = 2Y - P^2$

EQUATIONS

have $=$ signs
e.g. $y = 3x - 2$

REARRANGE

e.g. $y = 3x - 2$
    make x the subject

$x \rightarrow \times 3 \rightarrow -2 \rightarrow y$

$x \leftarrow \div 3 \leftarrow +2 \leftarrow y$

$x = \dfrac{y+2}{3}$

e.g. $3s = t^2 + 2$
    Make t the subject

$t \rightarrow sq \rightarrow +2 \rightarrow 3s$

$t \leftarrow rt \leftarrow -2 \leftarrow 3s$

$t = \sqrt{3s - 2}$

SOLVE

Find the letter

e.g.1
$$3m + 2 = 14$$
$$3m = 14 - 2$$
$$3m = 12$$
$$m = 12/3$$

$$m = 4$$

e.g.2
$$5x + 1 = 2x - 5$$
$$5x - 2x = -5 - 1$$
$$3x = -6$$
$$x = \dfrac{-6}{3}$$
$$x = -2$$

Test your knowledge 2

1   The travel graph below shows the journey taken by a motorcyclist.

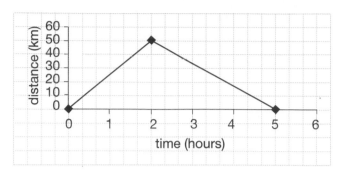

    a) Describe the motorcyclist's journey. [1]

    b) At what speeds did she travel? [1]

    c) What was her average speed for the whole journey? [1]

2   Find an expression for each sequence:

    a) 11, 14, 17, 20, 23, ... [1]

    b) 23, 20, 17, 14, 11, ... [1]

3   Solve the equations:

    a) $3(q - 2) = 24$ [1]

    b) $\frac{p}{2} + 6 = 12$ [1]

    c) $6s^2 + 1 = 7$ [1]

4   A rectangular garden has a width, w. The length of the garden is 2 m longer.
The area of the garden is 110 m^2.

    a) Show that $w^2 + 2w = 110$. [1]

    b) Find w to one decimal place. Copy and complete the following table.
A starting value for w has been done for you. [1]

w	$w^2 + 2w$		High/Low
9	$9^2 + 18$	99	L

5 Write down the equation of each line. **[3]**

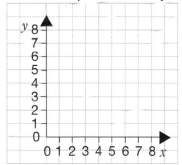

6 A line has equation $y = 3x - 1$. Complete the table of values below.
One has been done for you. **[1]**

x	−2	−1	0	1	2	3	4
y					5		

7 A line has equation $7x + 5y = 35$. Sketch the line on the axes provided. **[2]**

8 Simplify each expression:

a) $3y - 2 + 2y - 3$ **[1]**

b) $x^2 + y + 2x^2$ **[1]**

c) $3(2 + q) + (1 + 3q)$ **[1]**

9 The exchange rate between pounds sterling and US dollars is quoted as £1 = $1.93.
Calculate:

a) £345 in dollars **[1]**

b) $300 in sterling. **[1]**

(Total 21 marks)

Angle-land

Angles are everywhere.

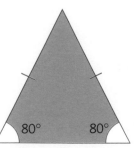

Here are some useful facts about angles.

This box means 90°

30°

60°

The angles in a triangle add up to 180°.

150°
30°

Angles on a straight line add up to 180°.

c
a
c
a

Alternate angles are the same (a).
Corresponding angles are the same (c).

160°
160°

Vertically opposite angles are the same.

30° 330°

Angles at a point add up to 360°.

80°   80°

Base angles of an isosceles triangle are the same as each other.

FURTHER PRACTICE

Here are some examples of how you find the missing angles. Make sure you understand each example.

1 $a + 60° + 80° = 180°$
$a = 40°$

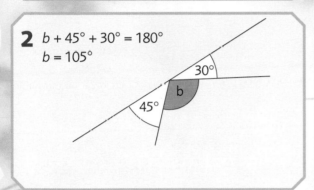

4 $d + d + 30° + 60° = 360°$
$2d + 90° = 360°$
$2d = 270°$
$d = 135°$

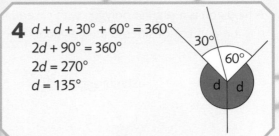

2 $b + 45° + 30° = 180°$
$b = 105°$

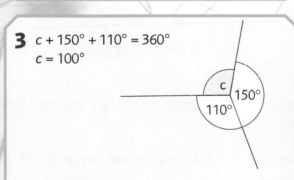

5 alternate angles:
$e = 50°$
$f + e = 180°$
$f = 130°$

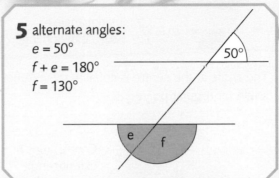

3 $c + 150° + 110° = 360°$
$c = 100°$

6 isosceles triangle:
$g + 70° + 70° = 180°$
$g = 40°$

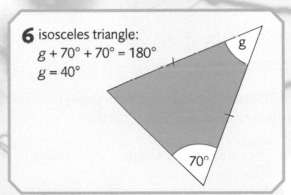

EXAMINER'S TOP TIPS

When two angles are labelled with the same letter (like example 4 above) in the same question, then they must be the same as each other.

KEY FACTS

180° total

Red angles are the same as each other. Grey angles are the same as each other.

360° total

180° total

Pretty poly

Regular shapes are everywhere.

A hexagon is a regular <u>polygon</u> with six equal sides. There are two important angles involved. *n* is the number of sides in the polygon.

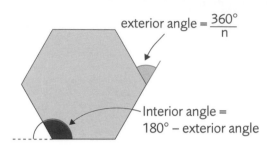

exterior angle = $\frac{360°}{n}$

Interior angle = 180° − exterior angle

Pretty Poly!

The angle at the centre is equal to the exterior angle for regular polygons.

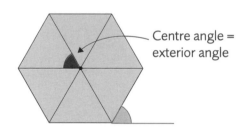

Centre angle = exterior angle

The table below shows these angles for various regular polygons. Have a good look and check that you agree with all the calculations.

regular polygon	shape	sides	exterior angle	interior angle	total of all interior angles
equilateral triangle		3	360 ÷ 3 = 120°	180 − 120 = 60°	60 × 3 = 180°
square		4	360 ÷ 4 = 90°	180 − 90 = 90°	90 × 4 = 360°
pentagon		5	360 ÷ 5 = 72°	180 − 72 = 108°	108 × 5 = 540°
hexagon		6	360 ÷ 6 = 60°	180 − 60 = 120°	120 × 6 = 720°
octagon		8	. . . . .	. . . . .	. . . . .

FURTHER PRACTICE

Look at how the table on page 46 can be completed.

A regular octagon has eight sides. To find the value of each internal and each external angle:

exterior angle = 360 ÷ n = 360 ÷ 8 = 45°
interior angle = 180 − exterior = 180 − 45 = 135°

A regular polygon has an interior angle of 160°. To find out how many sides this polygon has:

exterior = 180 − interior = 180 − 160 = 20°
exterior = 360 ÷ n = 20
360 = 20n
n = 18

Now try these questions for yourself (answers at the bottom of the page):

1 A ten-sided regular polygon is called a decagon. Find the values of its interior and exterior angles.

2 Find the sum of all the interior angles of a regular 12-sided polygon.

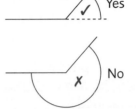

EXAMINER'S TOP TIPS

The exterior angle is between one side and the next side extended:

Yes

No

Don't make the common mistake of thinking it's all the way around the outside of a corner.

KEY FACTS

In general, for an n-sided polygon:

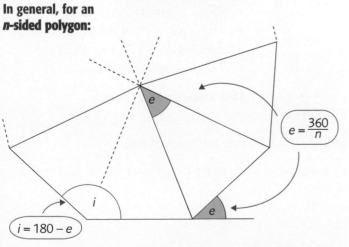

$e = \dfrac{360}{n}$

$i = 180 - e$

Answers

1 exterior angle = 360 ÷ n = 360 ÷ 10 = 36°
   interior angle = 180 − exterior = 180 − 36 = 144°

2 exterior angle = 360 ÷ n = 360 ÷ 12 = 30°
   interior angle = 180 − exterior = 180 − 30 = 150°
   12 interior angles, therefore sum = 12 × 150 = 1800°

Window cleaning

A window cleaner has been asked by the owner of a flat to clean her windows. He's not sure if his ladder will reach high enough.

Here's a simple way to work out how high up the block of flats the ladder will reach.

He has a ladder 5 m long. The closest he can get the bottom of the ladder to the block of flats is 2 m.

He constructs a triangle to scale using 1 cm to represent $\frac{1}{2}$ m. He does it accurately with ruler, <u>protractor</u> and <u>compasses</u>.
The method is:

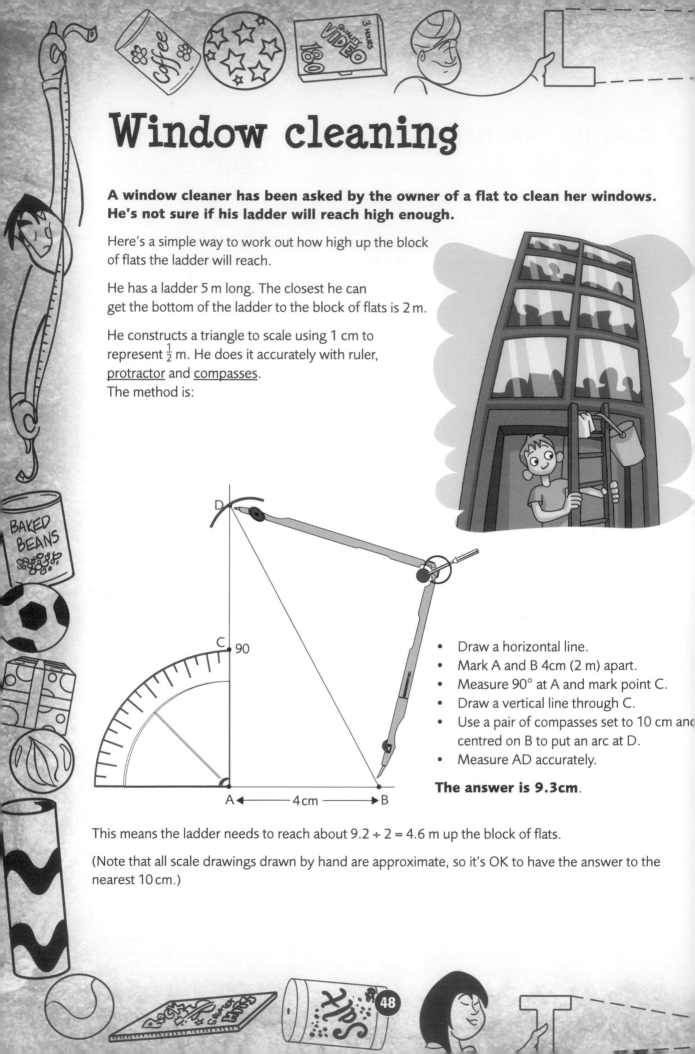

- Draw a horizontal line.
- Mark A and B 4cm (2 m) apart.
- Measure 90° at A and mark point C.
- Draw a vertical line through C.
- Use a pair of compasses set to 10 cm and centred on B to put an arc at D.
- Measure AD accurately.

The answer is 9.3cm.

This means the ladder needs to reach about 9.2 ÷ 2 = 4.6 m up the block of flats.

(Note that all scale drawings drawn by hand are approximate, so it's OK to have the answer to the nearest 10 cm.)

FURTHER PRACTICE

There are three main types of construction question, depending on what values you are given.

The diagrams show you how to do them. Follow the instructions and do all three on plain paper. This will build up your confidence and help you remember all three types.

1 Three sides known, e.g: 7 cm, 8 cm, 10 cm

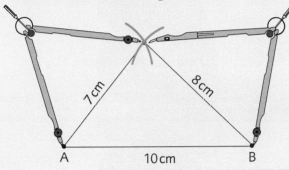

- Draw AB 10 cm long.
- Use a compass twice, making sure the arcs at 7 cm and 8 cm are accurate and intersect.

2 One side and the two angles at each end known, e.g. 7 cm, 40° and 60°

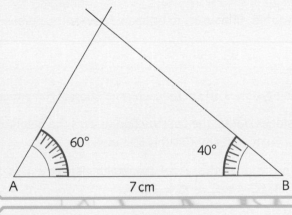

- Draw line AB 7 cm long.
- Use a protractor to measure and mark 40° at A and 60° at B.
- Extend protractor marks until they meet at C.

3 Two sides and an angle known,
e.g. AB = 8 cm, CÂB = 40°, BC = 5 cm

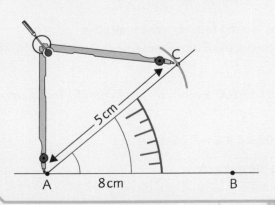

- Draw line AB 8 cm.
- From A measure 40° using a protractor.
- Extend a line from A along this 40° line.
- Use your compass set to 5 cm to put an arc on this line from B.
- Join B to C with a ruler.

KEY FACTS

There are three main types of question asking you to construct triangles:

- ☑ 3 sides known
- ➡ 1 side and the 2 angles at each end known
- ☑ 2 sides and an angle known.

On the treadmill

Castle builders in the Middle Ages often used a large wheel to hoist stones and equipment. It was driven by a man who walked around the inside of it – as hamsters do inside their wheels.

A health and safety inspector at Corfe Castle is worried. She wants to estimate how far the person in the wheel walks each day.

She estimates that the wheel's <u>radius</u>, r, is 1.4 m.

A rope attached to the wheel lifts a cradle containing stones 30 cm for each revolution of the wheel.

She estimates that the average height it lifts the stones during the construction work is the height of the castle – 10 m. This means the wheel turns 1000 cm ÷ 30 cm. Call this 35 turns.

To work out the distance the man walks around the inside of the wheel, the health inspector uses one of the equations for the <u>circumference</u> (C) of a circle: **C = πd, or C = 2πr**.

$$r = 1.4\,\text{m}$$

$$C = \pi \times d = 3.14 \times 2.8 = 8.792\,\text{m}$$

This distance is walked for each of the 35 revolutions. So the total distance walked is 35 × 8.792 = 307.72 m. Since she has already used estimates of the wheel size and castle height, she rounds this off to 300 m.

- At a walking speed of 0.5 m per second this would take 600 seconds or 10 min per lift. This means about 3 lifts per hour for an 8 hour day.

- The total distance walked in a circle is roughly 300 × 3 × 8 = 7.2 km per day.

She makes a note on her clipboard and moves on to the dungeons...

FURTHER PRACTICE

1 Find the circumference of each circle:

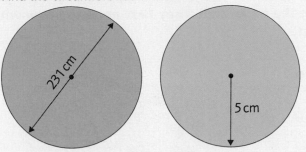

a) C = πd = 3.14 × 231 = 725 cm

b) C = πd = 3.14 × 10 = 31.4 m

2 Find the perimeter of each shape:

a) P = C/2 + 16 = (3.14 × 16)/2 + 16 = 41.1 cm

b) P = C/4 + 4 + 4 = (3.14 × 8)/4 + 4 + 4 = 14.3 m

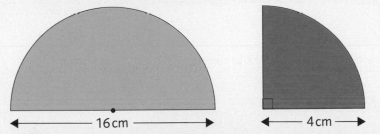

3 Now try this question on your own (answer at bottom of page):

A bicycle wheel has a diameter of 700 mm. How many times does the wheel turn for each kilometre cycled?

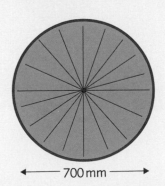

KEY FACTS

⬇ π is a constant used when dealing with circles and spheres. C/d = π, or C = π × *d*, or C = 2 × π × *r* for all circles.

➡ π = 3.14159265... but you generally use 3.14 to keep things simple.

Answers

3 700 mm = 70 cm = 0.7 m. C
= πd = 3.14 × 0.7 = 2.198 m
1 km = 1000 m. Wheel rotates
1000 ÷ 2.198 = 455 turns

Party hats

The Party Hat Company is designing a new line of cone-shaped party hats. To work out how much card to order from the paper mill, they first need to know what the area of the card is for a single hat.

The simplest cone is cut from card in the shape of three-quarters of a circle, as shown:

- The radius of the circle is 20 cm.

- The area of a circle is found using the radius:

  $$A = \pi r^2 = \pi \times r \times r$$

- For the whole circle of card:

  $A = \pi \times r \times r = 3.14 \times 20 \times 20 = 1256 \text{ cm}^2$

- For the $\frac{3}{4}$ circle cut to make the hat:

  $A = 0.75 \times 1256 = 942 \text{ cm}^2$

They now know the area of card so can work out how much paper to order from the mill to make ten thousand hats.

FURTHER PRACTICE

The first one has been done for you in each case.

1 Find the area of these circles:

a)

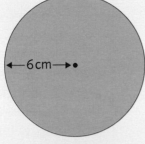
←6cm→•

$A = \pi r^2 = 3.14 \times 6 \times 6$
$= 3.14 \times 36 = 113 \text{ m}^2 \text{ (3sf)}$

b)

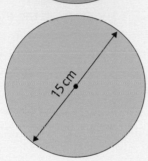
15 cm

2 Find the area of these shapes:

a)

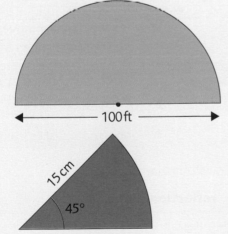
←—— 100ft ——→

half circle: $A = \dfrac{\pi r^2}{2}$

$= \dfrac{(3.14 \times 50 \times 50)}{2} =$

$\dfrac{7850}{2} = 3930 \text{ ft}^2 \text{ (3sf)}$

b)

15 cm
45°

KEY FACTS

⬇ **A = πr^2**

➔ **Square *r* first before multiplying by π.**

Answers

1b $A = \pi r^2 = 3.14 \times 7.5 \times 7.5 = 3.14 \times 56.25 = 177 \text{ cm}^2$ (3sf)

2b $\dfrac{45°}{360°} = \dfrac{1}{8}$ of a whole circle

$A = \pi r^2 \div 8 = (3.14 \times 15 \times 15) \div 8 = 3.14 \div 225 \div 8 = 88.3 \text{ cm}^2$ (3sf)

Showing the flag

Midshipman Marryat is a bit of a mathematician. When he's reading semaphore signals from another ship, he likes to work out the angle of rotation from one letter to the next.

He's saying, "my... arms... are... killing... me..."

Semaphore is a method of sending a message without the use of lights or radio (or mobile phone!). The position of two flags determines the letter of the alphabet being sent. It used to be a common way for ships to send messages between each other.

The positions of the flags for letters P and S are shown. As Midshipman Marryat looks at it, the top flag is rotated clockwise.

135°
S
P

When describing a **rotation** you must state three facts:

So when the signaller moves from letter P to letter S, Midshipman Marryat sees

1	the angle in degrees		1	a rotation of 135°
2	the direction (clockwise or anti-clockwise)		2	clockwise
3	the centre of the rotation.		3	about the signaller's head.

Rotation is only one kind of <u>transformation</u>. Other transformations include:

translation

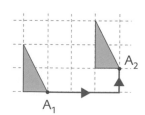

'three to the right, one up'

reflection

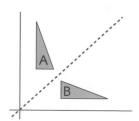

'reflection in the line $y = x$'

(**enlargement** – see pages 56–7)

FURTHER PRACTICE

Describe each of the transformations shown. The answers are at the bottom of the page.

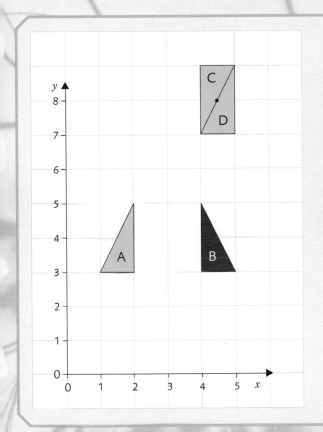

1 A to B

2 C to D

3 A to D

4 B to C

EXAMINER'S TOP TIPS

Don't make the mistake of writing 'transformation' when you mean 'translation'. A translation is only one of the four transformations.

Answers

1 A to B is a reflection in the line x = 3.
2 C to D is a rotation 180° about the point (4.5, 8).
3 A to D is a translation 3 to the right and 4 up.
4 B to C is a reflection in the line y = 6.
Note that you don't have to state the direction for a 180° rotation. It's the same either way!

Projecting an image

Slide projectors enlarge transparent photographs onto a large screen. The slide itself is a small picture 3.5 by 2.5 cm through which light is shone.

(a) 3.5 x 2.5 cm

(b) 1.05 x 0.75 m

The picture is enlarged by a *scale factor* (SF) so that it is easy to see.

$$\text{scale factor} = \frac{\text{enlarged length}}{\text{original length}} = \frac{\text{new length}}{\text{old length}}$$

Say the picture on the wall is 1.05 m across and 0.75 m high:
scale factor = 105 cm ÷ 3.5 cm = 30 (or 30:1)
or, using the height: 75 cm ÷ 2.5 cm = 30

There is another way to work out the scale factor if you know the distances from the *centre of enlargement* and points on the *object* and *image*. Here the centre of enlargement is the light bulb in the projector.

For equivalent points on object and image:

$$SF = \frac{\text{new distance to centre of enlargement}}{\text{original distance to centre of enlargement}}$$

Note: the original shape is sometimes called the <u>object</u>, and the enlargement is called the <u>image</u>.

FURTHER PRACTICE

1 In each diagram shape A has been enlarged to become shape B. What is the scale factor of each enlargement?

$$SF = \frac{B_1B_2}{A_1A_2} = 4\text{ cm} \div 2\text{ cm} = 2$$

$$or\ SF = \frac{CB_2}{CA_2} = 2\text{ cm} \div 1\text{ cm} = 2$$

$$SF = \frac{CB_1}{CA_1} = 6\text{ cm} \div 2\text{ cm} = 3$$

$$SF = \frac{B_1B_2}{A_1A_2} = 3\text{ cm} \div 1\text{ cm} = 3$$

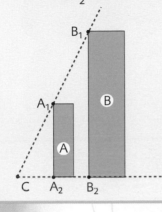
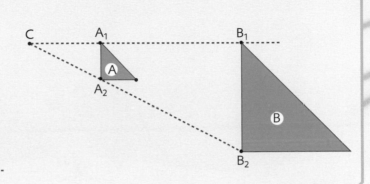

2 What is the scale factor using the information provided? The diagram is not drawn to scale.

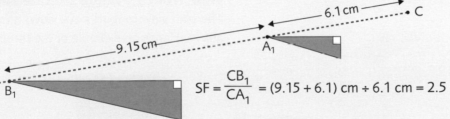

$$SF = \frac{CB_1}{CA_1} = (9.15 + 6.1)\text{ cm} \div 6.1\text{ cm} = 2.5$$

3 A photograph is 5″ high and 7″ wide. A picture frame has a maximum width of 9″. If the photograph is enlarged to fit the width, how high will the enlarged photo be?

$$SF = \frac{\text{new length}}{\text{old length}} = 9 \div 7 = 1.28...$$

$$\text{new height} = \text{old height} \times SF = 5 \times 1.28... = 6.4''$$

KEY FACTS

↓ $SF = \dfrac{\text{new length}}{\text{old length}}$

→ $SF = \dfrac{\text{new distance to centre}}{\text{old distance to centre}}$

EXAMINER'S TOP TIPS

Remember the two methods of working out the scale factor. You will need to use both, depending on the question.

Taking a view

Shapes cast different shadows depending on how they are held up to the light.

A cuboid casts different shadow depending on where the light comes from:

If an object is viewed from three directions at 90° to each other, these views are called **plan view**, **front <u>elevation</u>** and **side elevation**. The plan view (or bird's eye view) is from above. Here's an example of the three views:

FURTHER PRACTICE

1 Which groups of three views match which solid?

a) 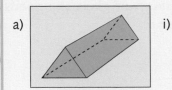   i)

b) 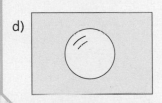   ii)

c) 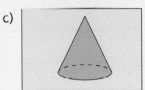   iii)

d) 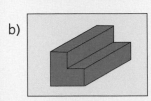   iv)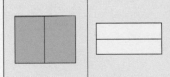

EXAMINER'S TOP TIPS

Be careful. Just because a solid has a circular cross section (e.g. a cylinder), this doesn't mean that all views of it are going to be circular.

2 Sketch all three views, A, B, and C, of the solid below. Indicate the dimensions on your sketches.

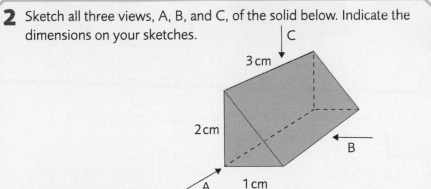

C

3 cm

2 cm

B

A   1 cm

KEY FACTS

⬇ **Plan view is from above.**

➡ **Elevations are from the sides.**

⬆ **The direction to be sketched is usually indicated by letters and arrows.**

Answers

1 (a) = (iii), (b) = (iv), (c) = (i), (d) = (ii)

2
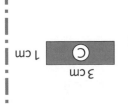

1 cm

2 cm

C

3 cm

1 cm

B

3 cm

2 cm

A

59

Rainbow wonder

Suzy Spector is a prism manufacturer. To work out the amount of glass she needs for her prism, she needs to calculate the volume of the prism.

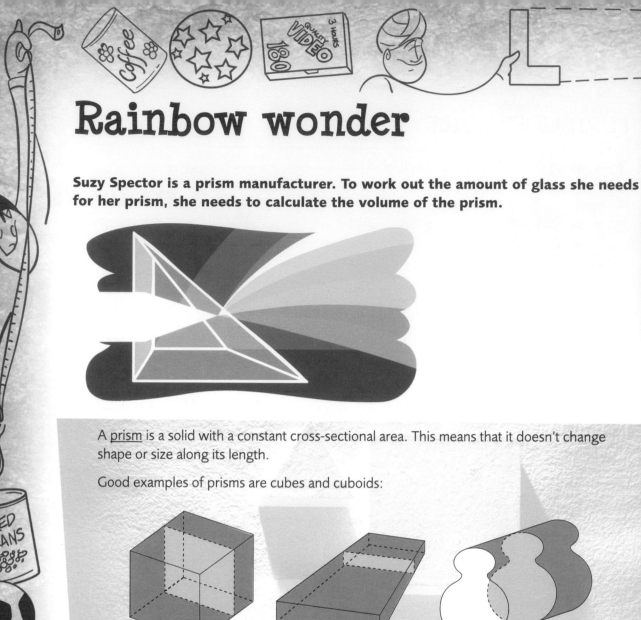

A <u>prism</u> is a solid with a constant cross-sectional area. This means that it doesn't change shape or size along its length.

Good examples of prisms are cubes and cuboids:

cube   cuboid   prism

The volume, V, of any prism with area or cross-section, A, and length, l, is found easily:

$$V = A \times l$$

These are the dimensions of Suzy Spector's prism:

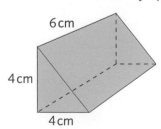

6 cm

4 cm

4 cm

To work out the area of a triangle:
$$A = \tfrac{1}{2} \times b \times h$$

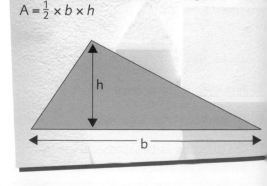

h

b

The cross-section is a triangle, so $A = b \times \dfrac{h}{2}$

$A = 4 \times \dfrac{4}{2} = \dfrac{16}{2} = 8 \text{ cm}^2$

so its volume $= A \times l = 8 \times 6 = 48 \text{ cm}^2$

FURTHER PRACTICE

Work out each volume carefully. Check each answer (at the bottom of the page) before doing the next one.

1 Work out the volume of each prism. Make your working clear.

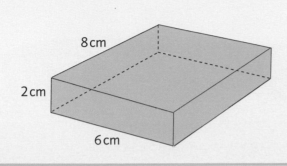
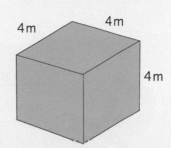

2 A cube has side 12.5 cm. Calculate its volume. Give your answer to 3 significant figures.

3 A right-angled triangular prism has dimensions as shown. Find the volume of this solid.

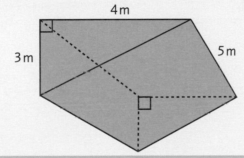

KEY FACTS

Volume of all prisms:

↘ $V = A \times l$ (A = area of cross-section, l = length)

↘ **The volumes of cubes and cuboids have simple equations:**

↖ volume of cube = $l \times l \times l$

↑ volume of cuboid = $b \times h \times l$

EXAMINER'S TOP TIPS

Remember that the units for volume will always be cubed (e.g. m^3, cm^3).

Net profit

A chocolate manufacturer wants to design a new form of packaging for its popular 'Crusher' chocolate bar. To see if the new packaging is cost effective, they need to work out how much card the package uses.

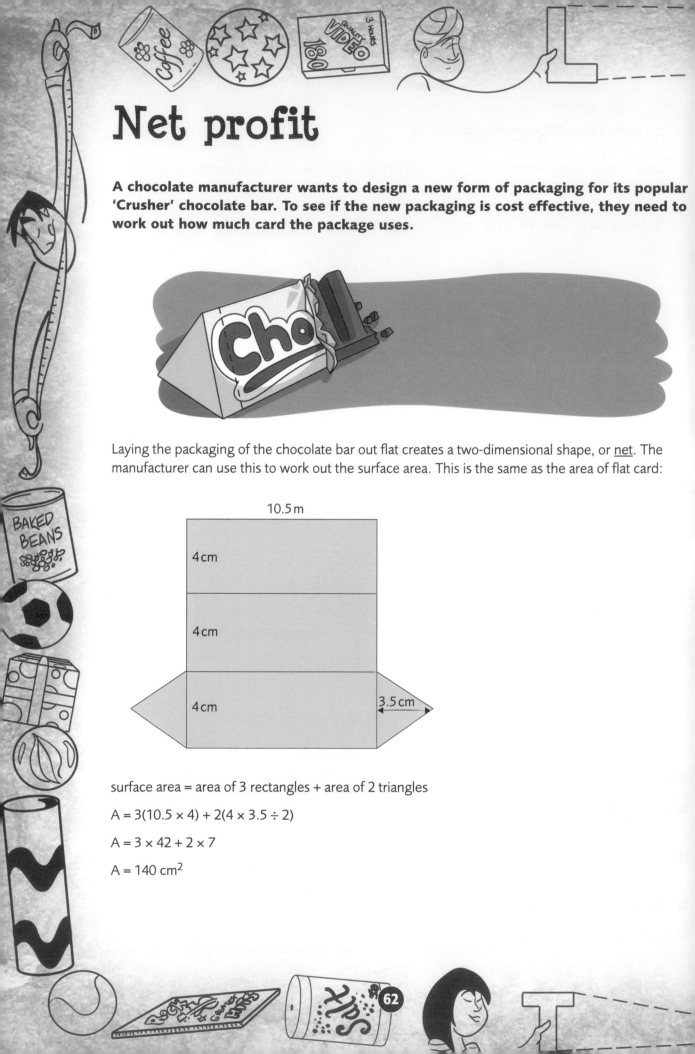

Laying the packaging of the chocolate bar out flat creates a two-dimensional shape, or <u>net</u>. The manufacturer can use this to work out the surface area. This is the same as the area of flat card:

surface area = area of 3 rectangles + area of 2 triangles

$A = 3(10.5 \times 4) + 2(4 \times 3.5 \div 2)$

$A = 3 \times 42 + 2 \times 7$

$A = 140 \text{ cm}^2$

FURTHER PRACTICE

1 A cube has six identical faces. All faces in a net of a cube are joined to at least one other face by an edge. Draw four nets of a cube. Two have been done for you.

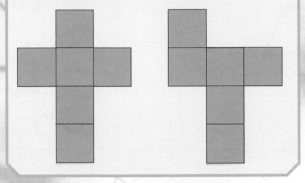

2

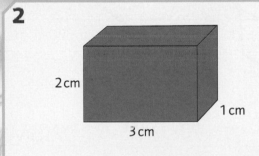

2 cm

1 cm

3 cm

a) Draw a net of the cuboid.

b) Find the surface area of the cuboid.

3

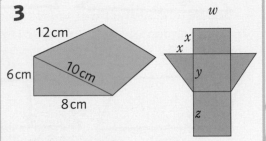

12 cm

6 cm

10 cm

8 cm

w

x
x

y

z

a) The shape and the net of a prism is shown. What are the lengths w, x, y and z?

b) Find the surface area of the solid.

EXAMINER'S TOP TIPS

Always draw a net before finding a surface area.

Make sure the number of faces on the solid equals the number of faces in your net.

KEY FACTS

The area of the net *is* the surface area.

Note these terms:

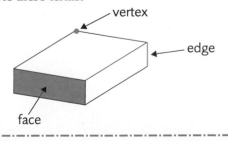

vertex

edge

face

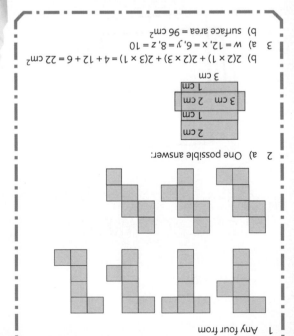

AREAS

$A = \dfrac{bh}{2}$

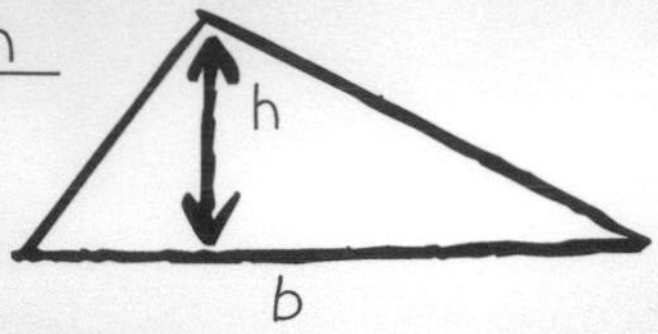

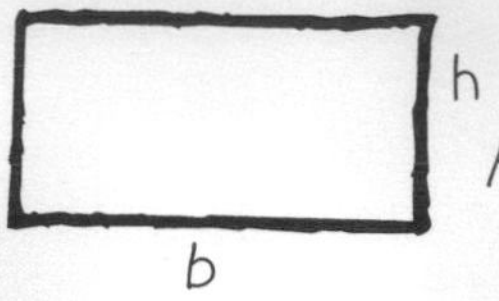

$A = bh$

$A = bh$

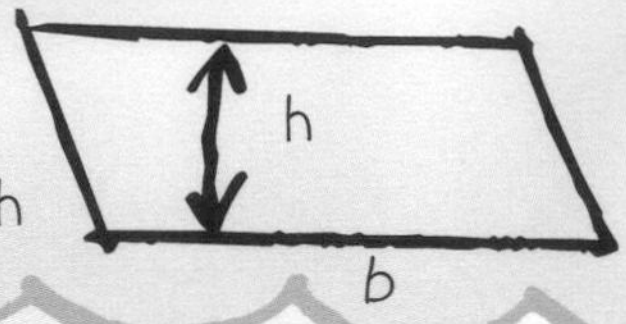

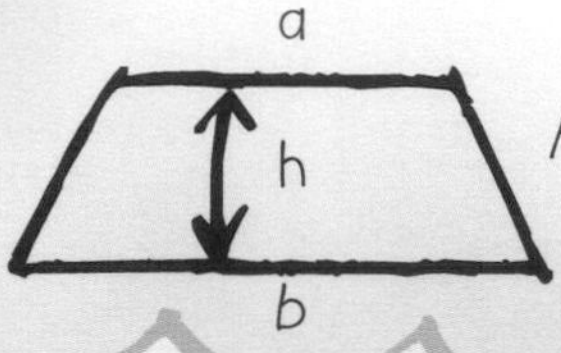

$A = \dfrac{a+b}{2} \times h$

SOLIDS

e.g. cuboid

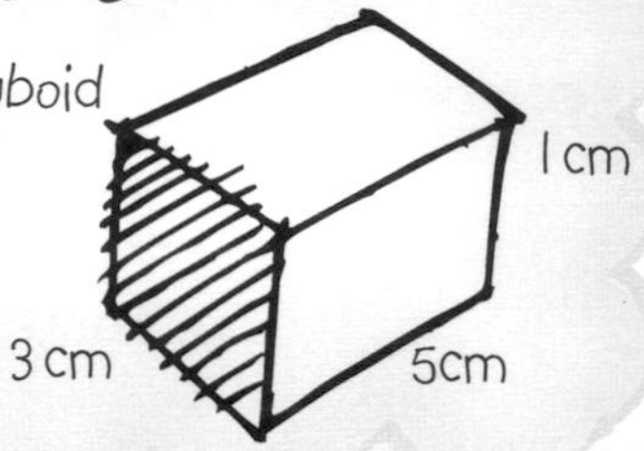

1 cm

3 cm   5 cm

NETS

e.g. cuboid

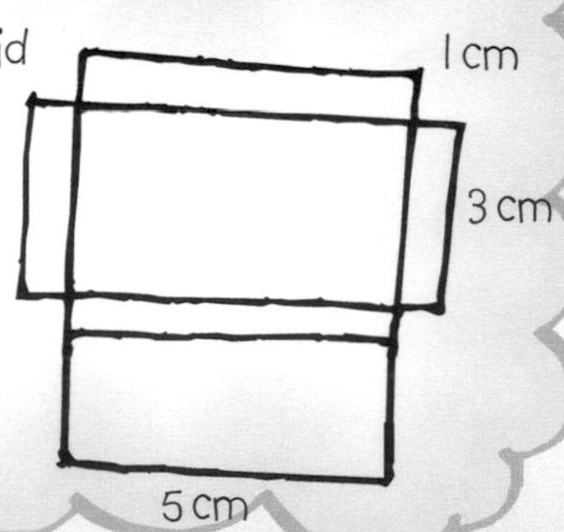

1 cm

3 cm

5 cm

VOLUME OF PRISMS

In general

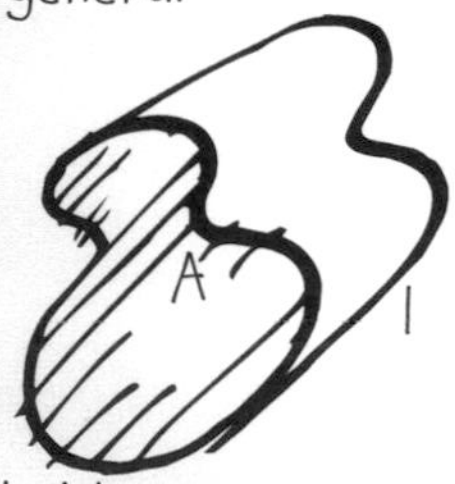

$V = A \times l$

Cuboid:
$A = 3 \times 1 = 3$
$V = A \times l$
$\quad = 3 \times 5 = 15\,cm^3$

SURFACE AREA

= area of net
e.g. cuboid
$2\,(5 \times 1) + 2\,(5 \times 3) + 2\,(3 \times 1)$
$= 10 + 30 + 6$
$= 46\,cm^2$

SH

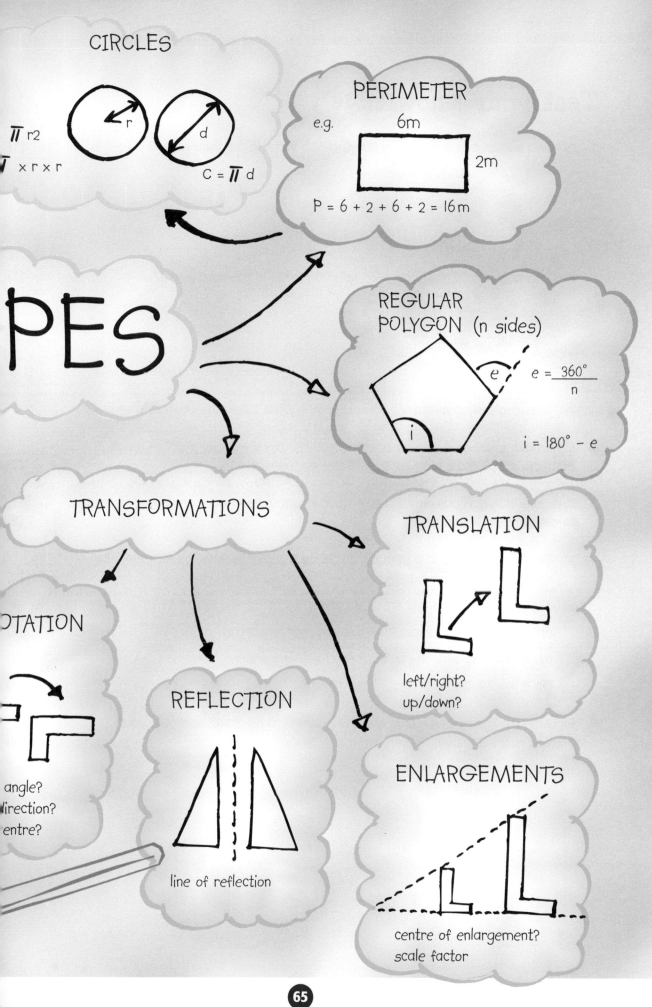

CIRCLES

$\pi r2$

$\pi \times r \times r$

$C = \pi d$

PERIMETER

e.g.

6m

2m

$P = 6 + 2 + 6 + 2 = 16m$

PES

REGULAR POLYGON (n sides)

$e = \dfrac{360°}{n}$

$i = 180° - e$

TRANSFORMATIONS

TRANSLATION

left/right?
up/down?

OTATION

angle?
direction?
entre?

REFLECTION

line of reflection

ENLARGEMENTS

centre of enlargement?
scale factor

Test your knowledge 3

1 a) Two angles in a triangle are 60° and 50°. What is the third angle?   [1]

   b) Two angles at a point are 160° and 90°. What is the third angle?   [1]

   c) One angle in an isosceles triangle is 50°. What could the other angles be?

2 On a plain piece of A4 paper accurately construct a triangle that has sides
   of 10 cm and 8.5 cm with an angle between them of 70°.   [2]

3 A regular polygon has nine sides. Find the sum of its interior angles.
   Show all your working.   [2]

4 a) Two of the angles in a triangle are 35° and 55°. Describe the triangle fully.
       Explain your reasoning.   [2]

   b) The angles in a triangle are $x°$, $y°$ and $x°$.

       (i) Describe the triangle fully. Explain your reasoning.   [2]

       (ii) Form, and simplify, an equation relating x and y.   [2]

       (iii) If $y = 20$, find x.   [1]

5 Find the perimeter of the shape shown. Take π to be 3.142 and give your
   answer to 3 significant figures.   [2]

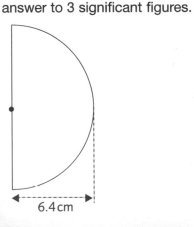

6.4 cm

6 Two circles of diameters 8 cm and 11 cm overlap. Together they form a shape to be used for a piece of jewellery. Find the area of the shape shaded. Take π to be 3.1 and give your answer to 1 decimal place. **[2]**

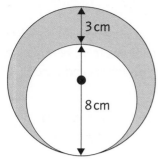
3 cm
8 cm

7 Describe the transformations which move each triangle onto the one indicated.

a) A to B **[1]**

b) B to C **[1]**

c) A to E **[1]**

d) A to F **[1]**

e) A to D **[1]**

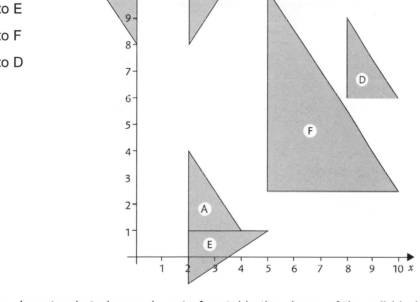

8 A heavy doorstop is to be made out of metal in the shape of the solid below. Calculate the volume of the solid. **[2]**

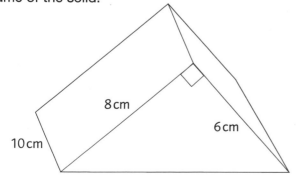
8 cm
6 cm
10 cm

9 A cube has a surface area of 96 ft². Find the length of each side. **[2]**

(Total 26 marks)

Postage puzzles

Wayne is catching up with his letter writing. He needs to work out exactly how much his letters and parcels will cost to send.

He refers to the two tables below, which he gets from the post office.

UK Letters and Parcels

Weight up to	1st Class	2nd Class
60 g	28p	21p
100 g	42p	35p
150 g	60p	47p
200 g	75p	**58p**
250 g	**88p**	71p

International Airmail: Small Packets

Weight not over	100 g	120 g	140 g	160 g	180 g	200 g
Europe	£0.98	£1.08	£1.18	£1.28	**£1.38**	£1.48
World	£1.31	£1.49	**£1.67**	£1.85	£2.04	£2.23

Wayne weighs his letters and parcels carefully, as follows:

A letter to Ronaldo in Brazil, **123 g**

A 1st class parcel to Wesley in Manchester, **249 g**

A letter to Ruud in The Netherlands, **165 g**

A 2nd class parcel to Thierry in London, **155 g**

He can now work out the total cost: £1.67 + £0.88 + £1.38 + £0.58 = £4.51

FURTHER PRACTICE

There are many different types of table that you may need to read from. The tables below show some weather data for Paris and Gibraltar from May to August. Check your answers at the bottom of the page.

Key: a = Average maximum daily temperature (°C)
       b = Average hours of daily sunshine (hrs)
       c = Average monthly rainfall (mm)

Paris	M	J	J	A
a	19	22	24	24
b	7	8	8	7
c	57	54	59	64

Gibraltar	M	J	J	A
a	23	26	28	29
b	10	11	11	9
c	25	4	1	3

1 How much hotter is the maximum August temperature in Gibraltar than in Paris?

2 What is the difference in May rainfall between Paris and Gibraltar, in centimetres?

3 How many more hours of sunshine does Gibraltar typically get in June than Paris?

EXAMINER'S TOP TIPS

Using a ruler to select the correct information from a table can help you to avoid making careless errors.

Read the key carefully. Sometimes columns or rows are totalled up in the last box: the heading will show if these are totals.

Make sure you know what units the table is using and what units the question is asking for. They're not always the same.

KEY FACTS

⬇ Sometimes columns or rows in a table are totalled up in the last box.

➡ Look at the heading to see if the column or row contains totals.

Film favourites

A GCSE Media Studies class has done a survey about favourite films over the last 50 years. Each student is asked to compare their preferences with two other students, and plot the results on scatter graphs.

The three scatter graphs below show the date of each film, and the mark out of ten given by each student.

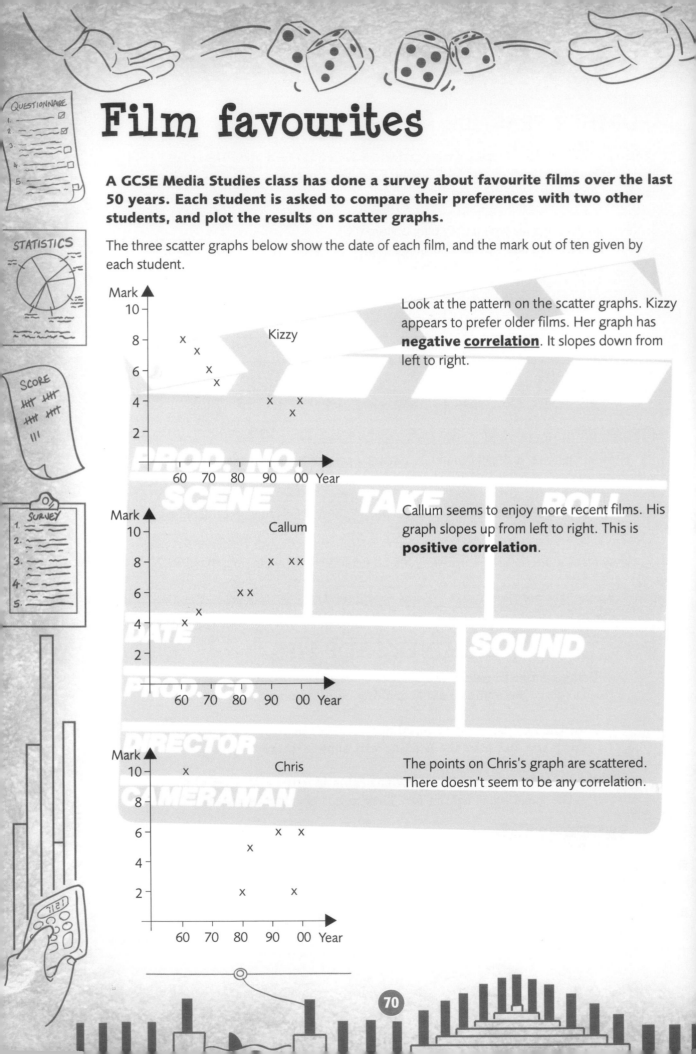

Look at the pattern on the scatter graphs. Kizzy appears to prefer older films. Her graph has **negative <u>correlation</u>**. It slopes down from left to right.

Callum seems to enjoy more recent films. His graph slopes up from left to right. This is **positive correlation**.

The points on Chris's graph are scattered. There doesn't seem to be any correlation.

FURTHER PRACTICE

Look at question 1 and make sure you understand the answer. Then try question 2 on your own (answers at the bottom of the page).

1 Describe fully the relationship between the quantities shown.

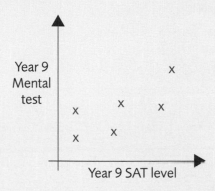

This is weak positive correlation. Generally the higher the students scored on the mental test, the higher the level they scored in the year 9 SAT overall.

2 In each case, describe and sketch the correlation that you would expect to see in a graph showing the measurements described.

a) An elephant's age against its weight.

b) The speed of a car and its fuel consumption in miles per gallon.

c) The age of a school girl against the length of her hair.

Answers

2a Strong positive correlation (age vs weight)

2b Strong negative correlation (speed vs fuel)

2c No correlation (age vs length)

Tombola Tim

Tombola Tim has a reputation for winning at raffles. That's because he can work out his chances of winning – he only takes part in a raffle if his chances are better than one in three.

In the latest raffle that Tombola Tim takes part in there are 90 different raffle tickets. Each is picked <u>randomly</u>. The prizes are:

- 5 holidays
- 10 bottles of wine
- 12 boxes of chocolates
- 6 cameras

The <u>probability</u> of an event happening depends upon the number of ways in which it can happen and the number of possible results in total.

$$\text{probability of event} = \frac{\text{number of ways of event happening}}{\text{total number of possible results}}$$

In this tombola, for the first prize won:

- probability of winning any prize = $\frac{(5 + 10 + 12 + 6)}{90} = \frac{33}{90} = \frac{11}{30}$

- probability of winning a camera = $\frac{6}{90} = \frac{2}{30} = \frac{1}{15}$

- probability of winning a bottle of wine or a box of chocolates = $\frac{(10 + 12)}{90} = \frac{22}{90} = \frac{11}{45}$

- probability of not winning any prize = $\frac{(90 - (5 + 10 + 12 + 6))}{90} = \frac{57}{90} = \frac{19}{30}$

Note that the probability of winning a prize $\left(\frac{11}{30}\right)$ and the probability of *not* winning a prize $\left(\frac{19}{30}\right)$ add up to 1 $\left(\frac{30}{30}\right)$.

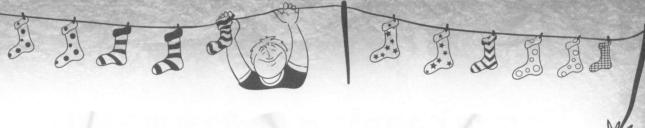

FURTHER PRACTICE

Look at the answer to question 1 and make sure you understand how it has been worked out. Then answer questions 2 and 3 on your own (answers at the bottom of the page).

1 A bag has only apples, bananas and pears in it. The probability of randomly taking out an apple is $\frac{1}{2}$, or taking out a banana is $\frac{1}{6}$. What is the probability of taking out a pear?

total probability is 1

therefore $\frac{1}{2} + \frac{1}{6}$ + prob. of pear = 1

$\frac{3}{6} + \frac{1}{6}$ + prob. of pear = 1

$\frac{4}{6}$ + prob. of pear = 1

prob. of pear = $1 - \frac{4}{6} = \frac{2}{6} = \frac{1}{3}$

2 Dai picks a weekday at random (Monday, Tuesday, Wednesday, Thursday or Friday).

What is the probability that the day of the week that he picks:

a)   has the letter 's' in it?

b)   has more than two vowels in it?

c)   has the letter 'y' in it?

d)   has the letter 'b' in it?

3 The probability of Stella being randomly picked for a particular part in the school play is $\frac{1}{8}$. What is the probability that Stella is *not* picked for the part?

EXAMINER'S TOP TIPS

Probability questions are usually asked using fractions, but don't be surprised if you see decimals occasionally. You still follow the same method.

KEY FACTS

⤓ probability of event = (number of ways event can happen) ÷ (number of possible results)

Housekeeping

This family keeps a record of how much they spend on housekeeping each month. It includes food, cleaning, all bills and maintenance. They record the figure for each month to the nearest £10.

These are the monthly figures over the whole year:

£1200	£960	£1050	£960	£1120	£980
£1100	£920	£960	£980	£1000	£1150

They want to work out the <u>average</u> monthly spending, but they aren't sure which average to use. They ask their neighbours to help them.

They explain that there are three different averages.

1 The *mode* is the **mo**st common value.
The most common amount spent is **£960**, as it occurs three times in the monthly records.
So the mode is **£960**.

2 The *median* is the middle value in size order:

920 960 960 960 980 **980 1000** 1050 1100 1120 1150 1200

There isn't a middle value here, because there is an even number of values. So you have to go half way between the middle pair:

(1000 + 980) ÷ 2 = **£990**
So the median is **£990**.

The *range* isn't actually an average. It measures the spread of the data.

range = largest value – smallest value

So for the months above:

1200 – 920 = £280
The range is £280

3 The *mean* is the **total of all values ÷ the number of values**.
The total monthly spending is £12,380.
There are 12 months recorded.
(12,380 ÷ 12) = **£1,030**
So the mean is **£1,030**.

FURTHER PRACTICE

Read through question 1 and check that you understand the three different averages. Then do question 2 on your own.

1 Oliver has recorded the number of boys and girls coming to the youth club over the last ten weeks. They meet once a week.

Boys	10	8	9	8	9	10	9	8	9	10
Girls	7	7	7	8	12	10	7	11	8	7

He now wants to work out whether boys or girls have a higher average attendance each week. He needs to check all three averages.

Mean

Boys: $\dfrac{(10 + 8 + 9 + 8 + 9 + 10 + 9 + 8 + 9 + 10)}{10} = \dfrac{90}{10}$. Mean = **9.0**

Girls: $\dfrac{(7 + 7 + 7 + 8 + 12 + 10 + 7 + 11 + 8 + 7)}{10} = \dfrac{84}{10}$. Mean = **8.4**

Median   **Mode**

Boys: 8 8 8 9 **9 9** 9 10 10 10. Median = **9**   Boys: 9 occurs most often. Mode = **9**

Girls: 7 7 7 7 **7 8** 8 10 11 12. Median = **7.5** Girls: 7 occurs most often. Mode = **7**

Which average is the best for Oliver to use? They are all the same for the boys. For girls the mode is the lowest number. This doesn't represent the girls' attendance. The girls' median is better but doesn't reflect the higher attendances (e.g. 10, 11 and 12). So the girls' mean is the best average to use.

Monday	6
Tuesday	7
Wednesday	9
Thursday	8
Friday	6
Saturday	8
Sunday	6

2 The seven days of the week are written out and the number of letters in each word is counted.

Find the mean, median and mode of the number of letters.

KEY FACTS

- **Mean** = total of values/number of values
- **Median** = middle number in order
- **Mode** = most common
- **Range** = biggest – smallest

EXAMINER'S TOP TIPS

Don't forget to put the numbers in order before working out the median. Many people do!

Answers

Mean = 7.1: $= \dfrac{\text{total}}{\text{number}}$

$(6 + 7 + 9 + 8 + 6 + 8 + 6) \div 7 = 50 \div 7 = 7.1$

Median = 7: in size order, letters in day are: 6 6 6 7 8 8 9

Mode = 6: most common number of letters is 6

Pie heaven

A bakery sells three types of pie. 40% of the pies are chicken and mushroom, 35% are steak and kidney, and 25% are vegetarian. The baker wants to show his sales on a pie chart, but how?

A pie chart is a circle divided up into **sectors**. The angles at the centre total 360°.

The baker's units are percentages, so he has to change this into degrees.

First he has to work out what 1 unit (1%) is worth in degrees.

Since 100% = 360°

then $1\% = \dfrac{360}{100} = 3.6°$

So $40\% = 40 \times 3.6° = 144°$

$35\% = 35 \times 3.6° = 126°$

and $25\% = 25 \times 3.6° = 90°$

Now all he needs to do is draw it.

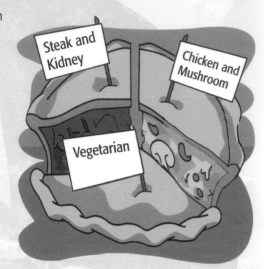

A pie chart has been drawn to show how many football fans support each of three teams. The angles are shown on the chart and can be used to work out what each sector represents.

Use the angles marked on the pie chart to find the fraction of the total in each case:

Carlisle Wanderers $= \dfrac{30}{360} \times 240 = 20$ fans

Gateshead United $= \dfrac{126}{360} \times 240 = 84$ fans

Newcastle Eagles $= \dfrac{204}{360} \times 240 = 136$ fans

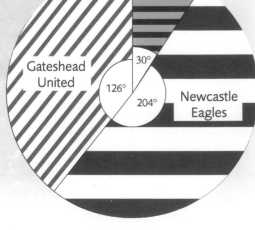

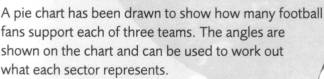

FURTHER PRACTICE

1 A school grades pupils' attendance each year from 'A' to 'D' (see chart). There are 1,440 pupils at the school. How many pupils are there with each grade? Show your working.

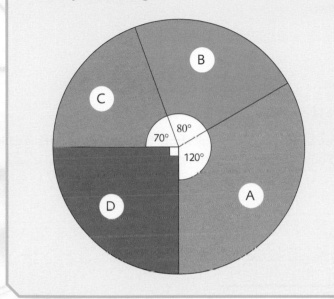

EXAMINER'S TOP TIPS

When you draw a pie chart make your angles accurate to the nearest degree or two. Use a sharp pencil and be careful to choose the correct scale on your protractor.

Be prepared to use a protractor to measure angles if you're not given the values.

2 Barry's hockey team won 12 games and lost 7. There were no draws. Draw a pie chart to represent these results. Show your working.

KEY FACTS

⬇ fraction of total = angle ÷ 360°

➡ angle = fraction of total × 360°

Answers

1 A: $\frac{120}{360} \times 1440 = 480$ pupils

B: $\frac{80}{360} \times 1440 = 320$ pupils

C: $\frac{70}{360} \times 1440 = 280$ pupils

D: $\frac{90}{360} \times 1440 = 360$ pupils

2 $12 + 7 = 19$ games in total. 19 games = 360°. 1 game = $360 \div 19 = 18.9... = 19°$

12 games ≈ $12 \times 19 = 228°$

7 games ≈ $7 \times 19 = 133°$

The 19° has been rounded up, so $228 + 133 = 361°$. This is 1° too much. It's best to take the 1° off the largest answer, so that you plot 227° and 133° on your diagram.

Dice dilemma

In the following dice game everyone rolls a dice at the same time, but each player uses the number shown on their dice differently.

- Player A takes their number and adds 5 to it.
- Player B takes their number and doubles it.

For example, if A rolls 4 and B rolls 5:

- A adds 5 to get a score of 9
- B doubles to get a score of 10 and wins.

Your task is to decide which player is more likely to win in the long run.

You need to draw up a table which includes all the possible results from the two events. This is called a <u>sample space</u>. It is very useful when two outcomes are to be compared.

Player A

	6	7	8	9	10	11
2	A	A	A	A	A	A
4	A	A	A	A	A	A
6	*	A	A	A	A	A
8	B	B	*	A	A	A
10	B	B	B	B	*	A
12	B	B	B	B	B	B

Player B

Key
A = win for player A
B = win for Player B
* = draw

The sample space shows all 36 possible results. There are 36 cells in the table.

You can see that Player A wins in 21 different ways.

The probability of Player A winning is therefore $\frac{21}{36} = \frac{7}{12}$.

This is over half. So Player A is more likely to win in the long run.

FURTHER PRACTICE

1 Two dice are rolled and the total of the two scores found. Look at the sample space below, which shows all the possible results:

Dice 1

Tot	1	2	3	4	5	6
1	2	3	4	5	6	7
2	3	4	5	6	7	8
3	4	5	6	7	8	9
4	5	6	7	8	9	10
5	6	7	8	9	10	11
6	7	8	9	10	11	12

Dice 2

a) What are the probabilities of:
  (i) the total being 4?
  (ii) the total being a <u>prime number</u>?

b) What is the most likely total?

2 A bag contains three purple sweets and two black sweets. One of the sweets is taken out at random. Its colour is noted before it is replaced. A sweet is taken out at random again.

Look at the sample space below, which shows all possible outcomes for the two sweets chosen.

2nd sweet

	P	P	P	B	B
P	PP	PP	PP	**PB**	**PB**
P	PP	PP	PP	**PB**	**PB**
P	PP	PP	PP	**PB**	**PB**
B	**BP**	**BP**	**BP**	BB	BB
B	**BP**	**BP**	**BP**	BB	BB

1st sweet

a) What are the probabilities that:
  (i) both sweets are black?
  (ii) the two sweets are different to each other?

Answers

1 (a) (i) $\frac{3}{36} = \frac{1}{12}$

  (ii) $\frac{15}{36} = \frac{5}{12}$

  (b) 7 occurs most often

2 (a) $\frac{4}{25}$

  (b) $\frac{12}{25}$

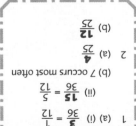

DATA

DATA SETS
eg. 5, 6, 3, 6

REPRESENTATIONS

RANGE
LARGEST – SMALLEST
6 – 3 = 3

AVERAGES

MODE

MOST COMMON

MODE = 6

MEDIAN

MIDDLE NUMBER

In order = 3, 5, 6, 6

$$\text{Middle} = \frac{5 + 6}{2} = 5\frac{1}{2}$$

$$\text{Median} = 5\frac{1}{2}$$

MEAN

$\dfrac{\text{TOTAL}}{\text{HOW MANY}}$

$$\text{Mean} = \frac{5 + 6 + 3 + 6}{4}$$

$$= \frac{20}{4}$$

$$\text{Mean} = 5$$

GRAPHS

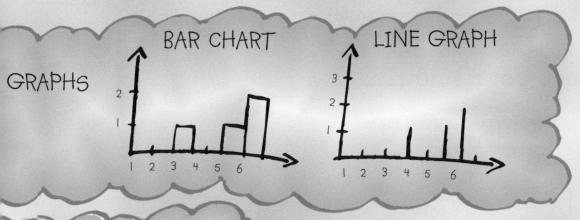

BAR CHART

LINE GRAPH

ΙE CHARTS

ANGLE

$$\text{ANGLE} = \frac{\text{Amount}}{\text{Total}} \times 360$$

$$\text{angle for 6s} = \frac{2}{4} \times 360 = 180°$$

PROBABILITY

PROBABILITY OF AN EVENT HAPPENING $=$ $\dfrac{\text{NUMBER OF WAYS EVENT CAN HAPPEN}}{\text{TOTAL NUMBER OF POSSIBLE RESULTS}}$

SAMPLE SPACE

BAG 1

BAG 2

one disc from each bag
taken out at random
B – Black
W – White
R – Red
Y – Yellow

BAG 2

BAG 1

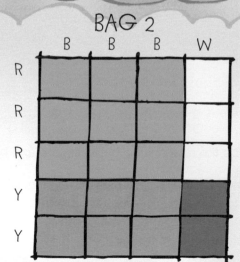

e.g. Probability of Red and Black disc $= \dfrac{9}{20}$

Probability of White and Yellow disc $= \dfrac{2}{20} = \dfrac{1}{10}$

Test your knowledge 4

1 Part of a distance chart is shown.

Bristol				
171	Cambridge			
44	203	Cardiff		
283	257	300	Carlisle	
206	124	238	400	Dover

The distance from Cambridge to Carlisle is 257 miles.

How much further is it from Bristol to Carlisle than from Carlisle to Cambridge? **[2]**

2 Uncle Jim has sown tomato plants every few weeks over the summer.
He has kept a record of their heights, in cm, each week:

age (weeks)	4	11	8	10	7	9
height (cm)	6	30	14	32	18	22

a) On the axes below draw a scatter graph of the data. **[1]**

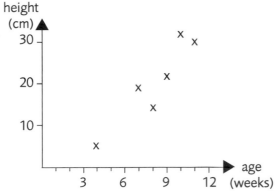

b) Describe the relationship between age and height. **[2]**

3 A fairground stall has a game where a spinner is rotated until it stops on one of the sectors shown. The possible prizes are shown in each sector.

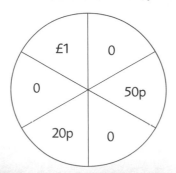

For each spin of the pointer, what are the probabilities that the player wins:

a) 50p [1]

b) nothing [1]

c) less than £1? [1]

4 a) Find the mean of these three numbers: 200, 400, 300. [1]

b) Find the median of the same three numbers. [1]

c) The mean of these four numbers is 250:

    200   x 400   300

Find the value of x. [1]

5 Two different dice, A and B, are rolled at the same time. The difference between the two numbers is worked out.

A/B	1	2	3	4	5	6
1		1			4	
2						
3	2					
4						
5						
6			3			

a) Complete the table. (Four differences have already been worked out for you.) [2]

b) What is the most likely difference? [1]

c) What is the probability that the difference is 2? [1]

6 A family spends a total of £86.40 per week on food. The pie chart below shows the proportion spent on each type of food:

Calculate how much is spent on each type of food. [2]

Practice paper

 Note: questions 1 to 6 are non-calculator questions

1

$\frac{1}{4}$	$\frac{1}{16}$ $\frac{1}{16}$	
	$\frac{1}{8}$	

The diagram may help you with the following questions.

Write down:

a) $\frac{1}{16} + \frac{1}{16} =$ .... **[1]**

b) $\frac{1}{16} + \frac{1}{16} + \frac{1}{8} =$ .... **[1]**

Calculate:

c) $\frac{1}{4} + \frac{3}{8} =$ .... **[1]**

2 Chris is making a large batch of strawberry jam and buys 17 lb of strawberries. 1 lb of strawberries costs £2.35.

How much does he spend? ....

Show your working. .... **[2]**

3 A variety box of crisps contains different flavoured packets.

2 packets   3 packets   4 packets   6 packets

There are 15 packets of crisps in the box altogether. One packet is taken out at random.

a) What is the probability that the packet is a plain one? .... **[1]**

b) What is the probability that the packet is either cheese or beef? .... **[1]**

c) What is the probability that the packet is not prawn? .... **[1]**

4 Calculate $\frac{4}{7} \times \frac{3}{8}$.

Show your working and write your answer as a fraction in its *simplest form*.

.... **[2]**

5 Solve:

a) $p + 6 = 18$ $p =$ .... **[1]**

b) $2q - 1 = 23$ $q =$ .... **[1]**

c) $3(5 + r) = 45$ $r =$ .... **[1]**

d) $2s^2 = 72$ $s =$ .... **[1]**

6 A triangle is shown with sides 6 cm, 7 cm and 8 cm.

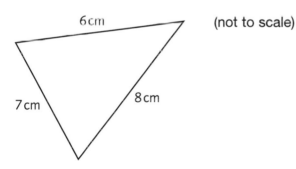

(not to scale)

In the space below, complete an accurate construction of the triangle. One side has been done for you. **[2]**

7

16	24	25

a) Work out the sum of 16 and 25. .... **[1]**

b) Work out the product of 16 and 25. .... **[1]**

c) What is the highest common factor of 16 and 24? .... **[1]**

d) What is the lowest common multiple of 16 and 24? .... **[1]**

8

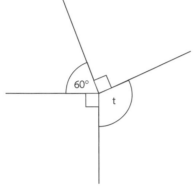

Not to scale.

a) Calculate the size of angle *t*. Show your working.

.... **[2]**

b) A regular polygon has an exterior angle of 90°.

Write down the name of this polygon. .... **[1]**

9 The graph shows a straight line.

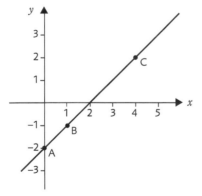

a) Fill in the coordinates of the three points indicated on the line AC:

A(..... , ...)

B(..... , ...)

C(..... , ...)   [2]

b) Write down an equation of the line.

.... [1]

c) On the graph draw the line with equation $x + y = 2$.   [1]

d) There are three transformations which each map the line AC onto the line with equation
$x + y = 2$. Describe each one fully:

(i) .... [1]

(ii) .... [1]

(iii) .... [1]

10 An employee is promoted. She earns an extra £2,315 per year. She pays 22% of this to the government in tax.

a) How much is 22% of £2,315?

Show your working.

.... [2]

b) She also pays £162 in National Insurance.

What percentage of £2,315 is £162? Give your answer to 2 significant figures.

Show your working.

.... [2]

11 24 pupils in a class were asked to choose their favourite radio station.

Station	Pupils
Radio 1	10
Radio 2	8
Radio 3	4
Radio 4	2

Construct a pie chart to represent this data. Use the circle provided.

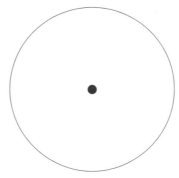

[2]

12 A factory makes cans for storing food. A cutting machine scratches a circular groove in the top of each can so that a ring pull will easily open the can. **[2]**

The radius of the groove is 2.4 cm. Calculate the length of each groove.

13 a) Suggest a way for the following sequence to continue.

1   3   9   ____   ____

(i) Fill in the next two numbers. **[2]**

(ii) Explain the rule that you have used in continuing the sequence. **[1]**

b) Suggest another way for the following sequence to continue. It must be different from the way you continued the sequence in part (a).

1   3   9   ____   ____

(i) Fill in the next two numbers in this sequence. **[2]**

(ii) Explain the rule that you have used in continuing the sequence. **[1]**

14 a) Find

(i) $\sqrt{169}$ **[1]**

(ii) $\sqrt{640.09}$ **[1]**

b) If $\sqrt{z} = 15$, what is z? **[2]**

15 One way of converting temperatures from degrees Fahrenheit (°F) to degrees Centigrade (°C) is to use the equation below.

$$C = \frac{5}{9}(F - 32)$$

Convert the following temperatures from °F to °C:

a) 68°F   **[2]**

b) 212°F   **[2]**

Convert the following temperature from °C to °F:

c) 0°C   **[1]**

(Total score for paper 53)

Glossary

Arc
Part of the circumference of a circle.

Average
There are three different averages:
- mean = total of the numbers ÷ number of numbers
- mode = most frequently occurring number. There may be more than one mode.
- median = the middle number when all numbers are placed in size order.

Circumference
The distance around the perimeter of a whole circle.

Compass
An instrument used to draw circles.

Correlation
The relationship (connection) between two sets of data often shown on a graph. The correlation may be strong or weak, or there may be none. Where there is correlation, it can be positive or negative.

Cube
A solid with six identical square faces and all edges of equal length.

A number generated by cubing an integer. The sequence of cubed numbers is often known as the 'cube numbers': 0, 1, 8, 27, 64 etc.

Cuboid
A solid with six rectangular faces. One pair of faces may be squares.

Denominator
The bottom number in a fraction.

Diameter
A line which goes through the centre of a circle and joins two points on the circumference.

Difference
The result of subtracting a smaller number from a larger number. The difference of 10 and 6 is 4.

Elevation
The side view of a solid. It is often described as a 'front' or 'side' elevation depending on where the view is taken from.

Equation
A mathematical relationship involving equality. There will always be an equals sign (=) in an equation.

Equivalent
Equivalent means equal. Equivalent fractions are equal to each other, e.g: $\frac{1}{3}$, $\frac{11}{33}$ and $\frac{2}{6}$ are all equivalent.

Estimate
Estimate means find a rough answer for a calculation. You will use approximate values for some or all of the numbers in the calculation.

Expand
Multiply out the brackets, e.g. $2(x + 3) = 2 \times x + 2 \times 3 = 2x + 6$.

Factor
A number that divides into another number a whole number of times, e.g. 4 is a factor of 12.

Form an equation
Make an equation up from the available information. You will use letters (e.g. x, y, t) when doing this.

Multiple
A number arrived at by multiplying another number by an integer, e.g. 8 is a multiple of 2.

Net
A two-dimensional shape which can fold up to make a solid.

Object and Image
When a shape is moved using a transformation, the original position of the shape is the 'object' and its new position is the 'image'.

Plan
The bird's eye view of a solid.

Polygon
A two-dimensional shape with straight sides enclosing an area, e.g. triangle (3 sides), square (4 sides), pentagon (5 sides), hexagon (6 sides), heptagon/septagon (7 sides), octagon (8 sides), nonagon (9 sides), decagon (10 sides).

Prime number
A number that has exactly two factors – itself and 1. 1 is not a prime number.

Prism
A solid with a cross section which does not change size or shape along its length. Cubes, cuboids and cylinders are all prisms. Cones, for example, are not.

Probability
The likelihood of an event happening, measured as a fraction, decimal or percentage, on a scale from 0 (impossible) to 1 (certain).

Product
The result of multiplying two numbers together. The product of 2 and 3 is 6.

Protractor
An instrument used for measuring angles.

Radius
The straight line or distance from the centre of a circle to a point on its circumference.

Random
Something done at random happens when the result isn't affected by the experiment or event itself. Picking similar sweets out of a jar without looking is random.

Sample space
A table which includes all the possible results from two events that occur simultaneously (e.g. rolling two different dice at the same time).

Sector
The area between two radii of a circle and part of the circumference.

Sequence
A number pattern such as 2, 5, 8, 11, where there is a relationship between each number and the next (e.g. +3).

Simplify
Combine elements of an algebraic expression so that the result is simpler. This may involve expanding/multiplying out brackets.

Solve
Find an answer to an equation.

Speed
The rate at which something is moving.
Speed = distance ÷ time

Substitute
Replace letters in an expression or an equation with numbers.

Sum
An addition. Finding the sum of two numbers means adding them up.

Symbol
A mark or sign that stands for something, e.g.:

$\equiv$	equivalent to
$\neq$	not equal to
π	pi, e.g. 3.14.

Transformation
There are four transformations: translation, rotation, reflection and enlargement. Each moves a shape from its original position to a new position.

Answers

Test your knowledge 1

1 a) $\frac{3}{4} \times \frac{5}{12} = \frac{3 \times 5}{4 \times 12} = \frac{15}{48} = \frac{5}{16}$

b) $\frac{3}{4} + \frac{5}{12} = \frac{9}{12} + \frac{5}{12} = \frac{14}{12} = \frac{7}{6} = 1\frac{1}{6}$

c) $\frac{3}{4} \div \frac{5}{12} = \frac{3}{4} \times \frac{12}{5} = \frac{36}{20} = \frac{18}{10} = \frac{9}{5} = 1\frac{4}{5}$

d) $\frac{3}{4} - \frac{2}{5} = \frac{15}{20} - \frac{8}{20} = \frac{7}{20}$

2 a) Increase 680 kg by 23%: $1.23 \times 680 = 836.4$ kg

b) Decrease £234 by 24%: $0.76 \times 234 = £177.84$

c) Increase \$203 by 3%: $1.03 \times 203 = \$209.09$

d) Decrease 346 g by 30%: $0.70 \times 346 = 242.2$ g

3 a) $3 + (4 \div 2) = 3 + 2 = 5$

b) $(3 + 4) \div 2 = 7 \div 2 = 3.5$

c) $(5 + 3) \div 2^2 + 1 = 8 \div 4 + 1 = 2 + 1 = 3$

d) $4(3 + 1) - 2 = 4(4) - 2 = 16 - 2 = 14$

4 a) $317 \times 491 \approx 300 \times 500 = 150000$

b) $1555 - 1492 \approx 1560 - 1500 = 60$

c) $125.3 \div 24.9 \approx 125 \div 25 = 5$

d) $1.82 + 14.82 \approx 2 + 15 = 17$

5 a) 23, 29, 31

b) e.g. 1 or 64

c) $48 = 12 \times 4 = 6 \times 2 \times 2 \times 2 = 3 \times 2 \times 2 \times 2 \times 2 = 3 \times 2^4$

d) $50 = 2 \times 5 \times 5 = 2 \times 5^2$
LCM $= 3 \times 2^4 \times 5^2 = 3 \times 16 \times 25 = 3 \times 4 \times 4 \times 25 = 12 \times 100 = 1200$

6 a) 18.02

b) 86.23

c) 85.176

d) 26.41

7 a) 3:4 = 7 shares. £343 $\div$ 7 = £49 per share
$3 \times 49 = £147$
$4 \times 49 = £196$
Check: £147 + 196 = £343 ✓

b) Sister A: 3 shares = £345, 1 share = 345 $\div$ 3 = £115
Sister B = $4 \times 115 = £460$

8 After 1 year account balance is $2000 \times 1.05 = £2100$

After 2nd year:	$2100 \times 1.05 = £2205$
After 3rd year:	$2205 \times 1.05 = £2315.25$

Alternative method: $2000 \times \mathbf{1.05 \times 1.05 \times 1.05} = 2000 \times \mathbf{1.05^3} = 2000 \times 1.\mathbf{1576}\ldots = 2315.25$ Interesting to note this is an increase of about **15.8**% altogether.

9 There are two values involved, one higher than the other. 10% is a fraction of the amount involved. 10% of the larger value is bigger than 10% of the lower value. For example, if the original value is £100 then a 10% increase leads to £110. Reducing this by 10% means taking off £11 (10% of 110 = 11) giving you £99.

10 a) $\frac{3}{7}$

b) $\frac{5}{7}$

c) $\frac{30}{49}$

11 a) 0.4

b) 40%

c) 64 kg

Test your knowledge 2

1 a) There are two parts to the journey. Both are at constant speed. The motorcyclist travels 50 km each way.

b) First part: 50 km/2 hr = 25 km/hr
Second part: 50 km/3 hr = $16\frac{2}{3}$ km/hr

c) Total distance = 100 km. Total time = 5 hr. Average speed = 100 km/5 hr = 20 km/hr

2 a) Gap = 3. For n = 4, 3n = 3 $\times$ 4 = 12. You want 20, so add 8.
3n + 8. Check: take n = 2, 3(2) + 8 = 6 + 8 = 14 ✓

b) Gap = −3. For n = 4, −3n = −3 $\times$ 4 = −12. You want 14, so add 26.
−3n + 26. Check: take n = 2, −3(2) + 26 = −6 + 26 = 20 ✓

3 a) $(24 \div 3) + 2 = 10$

b) $(12 - 6) \times 2 = 12$

c) $(7 - 1) \div 6 = 1$

   $s^2 = 1$

   $s = \pm 1$

4 a) area $= w(w + 2) = 110$

   $w^2 + 2w = 110$

b)

w	$w^2 + 2w$		high/low
9	$9^2 + 18$	99	L
10	$10^2 + 20$	120	H
9.5	$9.5^2 + 19$	109.25	L
9.6	$9.6^2 + 19.2$	111.36	H
9.55	$9.55^2 + 19.1$	110.30	H

$9.5 < w < 9.55$

Therefore w = 9.5 m (1dp)

5 a) $x = 5$

b) $c = -2$, $m = \frac{8}{4} = \frac{4}{2} = \frac{1}{2} = 2$

   $y = 2x - 2$

c) $c = 6$, $m = -\frac{6}{3} = -2$

   $y = -2x + 6$ (or $y = 6 - 2x$)

d) $y = 3$

6

x	−2	−1	0	1	2	3	4
y	−7	−4	−1	2	5	8	11

7

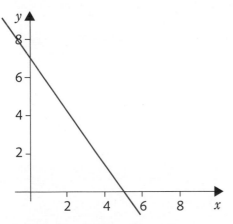

$x = 0$, $7(0) + 5y = 35$, $5y = 35$, $y = 7$

$y = 0$, $7x + 5(0) = 35$, $7x = 35$, $x = 5$

8 a) $3y - 2 + 2y - 3 = 5y - 5$

b) $x^2 + y + 2x^2 = 3x^2 + y$

c) $3(2 + q) + (1 + 3q) = 6 + 3q + 1 + 3q = 7 + 6q$

9 a) $345 \times 1.93 = \$665.85$

b) $300 \div 1.93 = 155.4401... = £155.44$

Test your knowledge 3

1 a) Angles total 180°, so 180 − 60 − 50 = 70°.

b) Angles total 360°, so 360 − 160 − 90 = 110°

c) You don't know whether the 50° given is a base angle or not, so there are two possible answers:

   (i) 50° is a base angle. Therefore the other angles are 50° and (180 − 50 − 50) = 80°.

   (ii) 50° isn't a base angle. Therefore the other angles both are. Each will be (180 − 50) ÷ 2 = 130 ÷ 2 = 65°.

2

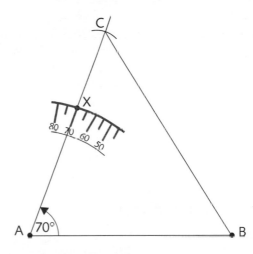

Draw line AB 10 cm long.

Measure angle with protractor 70° from line AB.

Mark X at 70°.

Draw line AX extended.

Mark arc, centre A, 8.5 cm, at C.

Draw BC.

3 n = 9

exterior angle = 360 ÷ 9 = 40°

interior angle = 180 − 40 = 140°

sum of interior angles = 140 × n = 140 × 9 = 1260°

4 a) 35° + 55 = 90°

The third angle will be 180° − 90° = 90°.

Therefore the triangle is a right-angled one.

b) (i) Since two angles are the same, and the third different, the triangle is isosceles.

   (ii) $x + x + y = 180$, $2x + y = 180°$

   (ii) $2x + 20 = 180$, $2x = 160$, $x = 80°$

5 $P = \pi d \div 2 + d$
$d = 6.4 \times 2 = 12.8$ cm
$P = \pi \times 12.8 \div 2 + 12.8 = 32.9088 = 32.9$ cm (3sf)

6 larger circle: $r = 5.5$
smaller circle: $r = 4$
total area $= \pi \times 5.5^2 - \pi \times 4^2$
$= 30.25\pi - 16\pi$
$= 14.25\pi$
$= 44.175 = 44.2$ cm^2

7 a) reflection in the line $y = 6$
b) reflection in the line $x = 1$
c) rotation, 90°, clockwise, about the point (2,1)
d) enlargement, centre (0,0), scale factor $2\frac{1}{2}$
e) translation 6 right and 5 up

8 triangular prism
area of cross section $= bh/2 = (8 \times 6) \div 2 = 48 \div 2$
$= 24$ cm^2
volume $= A \times l = 24 \times 10 = 240$ cm^3
Notice you didn't need to know the longest side
of the triangular face.

9 Cube has 6 identical sides, length l. SA $= 6l^2$
$6l^2 = 96$, $l^2 = 16$, $l = 4$ cm

Test your knowledge 4

1 Bristol – Carlisle = 283 miles
Carlisle – Cambridge = 257 miles.
difference = 283 – 257 = 26 miles

2 a)

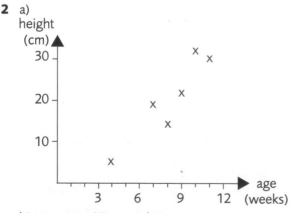

b) strong positive correlation

3 a) $\frac{1}{6}$

b) $\frac{3}{6} = \frac{1}{2}$

c) $\frac{5}{6}$

4 a) $(200 + 300 + 400) \div 3 = 900 \div 3 = 300$
b) in order: 200 300 400, median = 300
c) $\frac{(200 + x + 400 + 300)}{4} = 250$
$200 + x + 400 + 300 = 1000$
$900 + x = 1000$
$x = 100$

5 a)

A/B	1	2	3	4	5	6
1	0	1	2	3	4	5
2	1	0	1	2	3	4
3	2	1	0	1	2	3
4	3	2	1	0	1	2
5	4	3	2	1	0	1
6	5	4	3	2	1	0

b) 1
c) $\frac{8}{36} = \frac{4}{18} = \frac{2}{9}$

6 dairy: $\frac{90°}{360°} \times 86.40 = \frac{1}{4} \times 86.40 = £21.60$

meat: $\frac{160°}{360°} \times 86.40 = \frac{4}{9} \times 86.40 = £38.40$

groceries: $\frac{110°}{360°} \times 86.40 = \frac{11}{36} \times 86.40 = £26.40$

check: £21.60 + £38.40 + £26.40 = £86.40 ✓

Practice paper answers

1 a) $\frac{1}{16} + \frac{1}{16} = \frac{2}{16} = \frac{1}{8}$ **[1]**

b) $\frac{1}{16} + \frac{1}{16} + \frac{1}{8} = \frac{4}{16} = \frac{1}{4}$ **[1]**

c) $\frac{1}{4} + \frac{3}{8} = \frac{2}{8} + \frac{3}{8} = \frac{5}{8}$ **[1]**

2 $2.35 \times 17 = £39.95$ **[2]**

You must show your working clearly. This should make it obvious how you have done the calculation without a calculator.
Two possible methods are:

(i) 2.**35**
    1 7 ×
16²4³5
  2350
39.**95**

(ii) 10 lb = 23.50 = 23.50
5 lb = 23.50 ÷2 = 11.75
2 lb = 23.50 ÷ 5 = 4.70 +
17 lb = 39.95

3 a) $\frac{2}{15}$ **[1]**

b) $\frac{10}{15} = \frac{2}{3}$ **[1]**

c) $\frac{12}{15} = \frac{4}{5}$ **[1]**

4 $\frac{4}{7} \times \frac{3}{8} = \frac{12}{56} = \frac{6}{28} = \frac{3}{14}$ **[1]**

5 a) $p = 18 - 6 = 12$ **[1]**
b) $q = (23 + 1) \div 2 = 12$ **[1]**
c) $r = (45 \div 3) - 5 = 10$ **[1]**
d) $s^2 = (72 \div 2) = 36$, $s = 6$ or -6 **[1]**

6

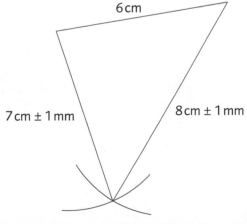

6 cm

7 cm ± 1 mm   8 cm ± 1 mm

[2]

7 a) $16 + 25 = 41$ **[1]**
b) $16 \times 25 = 4 \times 4 \times 25 = 4 \times 100 = 400$ **[1]**
c) 8 **[1]**
d) $16 = 2^4$, $24 = 3 \times 2^3$, LCM $= 3 \times 2^4 = 48$ **[1]**

8 a) $t + 90 + 90 + 60 = 360$
$t + 240 = 360$
$t = 360 - 240 = 120°$ **[2]**
b) square **[1]**

9 a) A (0, -2), B (1, –1), C (4, 2) **[2]**
b) $y = x - 2$ **[1]**
c) **[1]**

d) (i) reflection in the x axis ($y = 0$) **[1]**
  (ii) reflection in the line x = 2 **[1]**
  (iii) rotation 90° (clockwise or anti-clockwise) about the point (2, 0) **[1]**

10 a) 22% of £2315 = 0.22 × 2315 = £509.30 **[2]**
b) $(\frac{162}{2315}) \times 100 = 0.0699... \times 100 = 6.99...$
$= 7.0$ (2sf) **[2]**

11 24 pupils, 360°, therefore 1 pupil $= \frac{360}{24} = 15°$
Radio 1 = 150°, Radio 2 = 120°,
Radio 3 = 60°, Radio 4 = 30° **[2]**

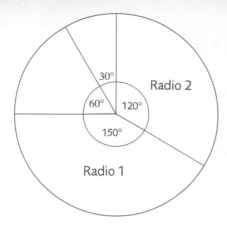

(angles accurate to +/− 2°)

12 $C = \pi d = 2 \times \pi \times 2.4 = 4.8 \times 3.14 = 15.072 = 15.1$ cm

13 a) (i) 1, 3, 9, 19,.33 **[2]**

     (ii) The first two 'gaps' are 2 and 6. These have a difference of 4. Using an increase of 4 in each gap means the next gaps are 10 and 14. **[1]**

   b) (i) 1, 3, 9, 27, 81 **[2]**

     (ii) Each term is three times the previous one. **[1]**

NB Answers to a) and b) can be in either order.

14 a) (i) 13 **[1]**

     (ii) 25.3 **[1]**

   b) $z = 15^2 = 225$ **[2]**

15 a) $C = \frac{5}{9}(68 - 32) = \frac{5}{9}(36) = 20°C$ **[2]**

   b) $C = \frac{5}{9}(212 - 32) = \frac{5}{9}(180) = 100°C$ **[2]**

   c) $0 = \frac{5}{9}(F - 32)$. For the right hand side to be equal to zero the bracket must equal zero. $F - 32 = 0$. $F = 32°F$. **[1]**